"Robert Firestone, clearly one of the most influen~~~~ generation, and Tamsen Firestone, ha~~~ *Love*. This book is the definitive guide i relationships. Since the text is packed fr journal exercises, it is a wonderful refe clients who can use it for bibliotherapy. individuals need to stop pushing away lo ~~ook provides a wealth of useful interventions."

— **Howard Rosenthal, EdD**, author of *Encyclopedia of Counseling* and *Encyclopedia of Human Services*

"*Daring to Love* is a wonderfully wise, beautifully written, and eminently practical book for anyone wishing to establish and maintain deeper, richer, and more lasting close relationships. It distills decades of research and clinical experience aimed at understanding and overcoming personal and relational barriers to happy, psychologically healthy living. The book contains many useful, personally engaging exercises based on the authors' voice therapy, organized around specific barriers to intimacy. As a relationship researcher who frequently writes about attachment theory and close relationships, I receive numerous requests for books that help a person overcome relationship problems. *Daring to Love* will now be on my short list of enthusiastic recommendations."

— **Phillip R. Shaver, PhD,** distinguished professor of psychology emeritus, University of California, Davis; coeditor of *Handbook of Attachment*; and coauthor of *Adulthood*

"This book invites us into raw vulnerability only made possible by the competent, compassionate hands of two authors who have lived—and loved—the principles they set forth. Perhaps the last paragraph of this book explains why it deserves to be read, integrated, and actualized into practice: '*Love is worth believing in.* Love is worth fighting for. Love is worth the personal challenge. No other endeavor offers higher rewards.'"

— **Pat Love, EdD, LMFT,** author of *The Truth About Love*

DARING
TO
LOVE

move beyond fear *of* intimacy,
embrace vulnerability,
and
create lasting connection

TAMSEN FIRESTONE
with **ROBERT W. FIRESTONE**, PʜD

New Harbinger Publications, Inc.

Publisher's Note

This publication is designed to provide accurate and authoritative information in regard to the subject matter covered. It is sold with the understanding that the publisher is not engaged in rendering psychological, financial, legal, or other professional services. If expert assistance or counseling is needed, the services of a competent professional should be sought.

Distributed in Canada by Raincoast Books

Copyright © 2018 by Tamsen Firestone and Robert W. Firestone
New Harbinger Publications, Inc.
5674 Shattuck Avenue
Oakland, CA 94609
www.newharbinger.com

Cover design by Amy Shoup

Edited by Xavier Callahan

Library of Congress Cataloging-in-Publication Data on file

20   19   18

10   9   8   7   6   5   4   3   2   1   First Printing

Being deeply loved by someone gives you strength,
while loving someone deeply gives you courage.

—Lao Tzu

This book is dedicated to each of you who,
with strength and courage, is daring to love.

Contents

Foreword

Immature love says: *"I love you because I need you."*
Mature love says: *"I need you because I love you."*

—Erich Fromm, *The Art of Loving*

Emotions are fundamentally relational—they link us to each other—so any relationship is a wellspring of emotional experience. But in order to be intimate with a partner in a love relationship, we have a special need to manage our emotions wisely.

Once we are aware of what we feel, our emotions give us information about whether an intimate bond is in good condition or in need of maintenance. We are calm and feel good when all is going well between us, and we are disturbed and upset when all is not well.

As human beings, we have been primed by evolution to have pleasant feelings when we are close to others and when we are recognized and valued by others, and this was especially so with respect to our caregivers during childhood. Today, as adults seeking to form healthy attachments and intimate relationships, we find that we continue to depend on emotional availability along with responsiveness, security, and warmth. We need others in order to feel secure and happy.

We feel secure in our love relationships when we have the closeness we need. Another important element is attraction, liking, and romantic passion. Warmth, liking, and appreciation of the other comprise a distinct aspect of the bonding system. We all seek and desire our partners for our excitement, interest, and joy in who they are.

But when we don't deal with our emotions and express our needs, negative patterns of interaction develop. The primary vulnerable emotions that underlie the threats to healthy attachment are fear of being unable to survive on our own and sadness at the possible loss of the comfort provided by our loved one. Another primary vulnerable feeling that can arise in a love relationship comes from threats to our identity and self-esteem. We feel worthy (that is, we feel pride) when we are recognized and validated by our partner, and we experience unpleasant feelings of shame or powerlessness when we are ignored or controlled. In this way, feelings of shame from threats to our identity and self-esteem can become central to how we feel about our partner.

Thus, conflict between partners emerges from continuing but unmet needs in adulthood for attachment, identity (or self-esteem), and affection. At the same time, the problem between the partners is not the particular needs that one or both of them may have. The problem is either fear of expressing those needs or the way in which the frustration of those needs is being managed. The solution is not for one partner to try to get his or her needs met by forcing the other to change. The solution is for both partners to reveal themselves to each other, forgive each other for being different, and have compassion for each other. To resolve their conflict, they need to be able to reveal their essential selves to each other and be accepted as they are—to be seen and known.

To develop mature love, as characterized by Erich Fromm, we need first to be aware of our attachment- and identity-related feelings and needs and then to communicate them to our partner in nondemanding ways (Greenberg & Goldman 2008). As Martin Buber has said, intimacy, once lost, can be regained only through the partners' revelation of the "Thou" to one another in an "I-Thou" form of dialogue. Intimacy, then, is about trusting our partner enough, and feeling safe enough with our partner, to reveal our vulnerability and engage in dialogue while also being strong enough to state our needs, set boundaries when we need to, and soothe ourselves when our partner is not available.

All of this depends on a special type of emotional competence. In *Daring to Love*, Tamsen and Robert Firestone lead you, the reader, through a process that will take you from immature love to mature love. They clearly lay out the way in which long-established systems of protection, once necessary, operate in the present to cut people off from experiencing love. The book is rich in exercises to help readers identify defenses as well as attachment- and identity-preserving patterns from childhood, patterns that interfere today with romantic relationships. The authors also highlight the way in which the critical, attacking voice that most of us carry in our heads—a type of alien self made up of destructive attitudes and defenses left over from our formative years—constantly gets in the way of openness and intimacy, works against our personal development, opposes our best interests, diminishes our sense of self, and sabotages our love relationships. But the authors don't stop there. They go on to give you methods for challenging that voice, help you examine what you may be doing to keep from being vulnerable, and guide you in exploring what you can do to become more vulnerable as you learn to establish and maintain greater closeness and intimacy. In short, this book will help you reveal your vulnerable "Thou" to your partner and set you on the path to mature love.

—Leslie Greenberg
Toronto
August 2017

Introduction

A coward is incapable of exhibiting love; it is the prerogative of the brave.

—Mohandas K. Gandhi, presidential address to the First Gujarat Political Conference, November 3, 1917

All you need is love. While each of us would probably wholeheartedly agree with this sentiment, why is it that so many of us struggle to maintain a loving relationship in our lives? It seems that although true love may be somewhat hard to find, it is even more difficult for many of us to accept and tolerate.

So what goes wrong? What gets in the way of our being able to have the one thing that brings us the most gratification and imbues our lives with the most meaning?

This book explains why and how we often, without awareness, act contrary to our best interests by reacting against love. The book also reveals how our habits of emotional self-defense interfere with our ability to give and receive love. When we are hurt or suffer psychological pain or trauma in growing up, we develop suspicious and distrustful, even fearful, attitudes about love and relationships. We attempt to protect ourselves from getting hurt again by developing a series of defensive strategies. This book will help you understand how these underlying defenses drive your actions, and it will offer you a method for challenging them. Both your understanding of your defenses and your ability to challenge them will enable you to overcome your psychological obstacles to love.

No one has ever said that love is easy! Part of the problem is that we don't recognize love as a skill that can be learned and developed. We often treat it as if it were an instinct or an innate ability. We think that loving should be second nature, like breathing, so when we find that it is not, we feel hopeless and give up instead of realizing that the time has come for us to get to work and develop our ability to love. Most of us are understandably reluctant to explore the reasons why we reject love, or to examine the barriers we inadvertently erect against closeness and intimacy. It is truly a brave act to look deeply into yourself, investigate your defenses and limitations, and then confront and change them. But it is a truly worthwhile endeavor.

How This Book Came About

For more than thirty years, the two of us, Tamsen and Robert Firestone, have been participating in discussion groups and workshops focused on couple relationships and personal development. In the 1990s, Tamsen edited Robert's book *Fear of Intimacy* (Firestone & Catlett 1999), and since then she has worked with him as an editor on his many books and articles for mental health professionals. After the turn of the twentieth century, she created PsychAlive: Psychology for Everyday Life (www.psychalive.org), a website where information originally made available to academics and professionals in psychology has been converted into articles that a layperson can easily understand. PsychAlive focuses on Robert's psychological theory and also includes material from other theorists and researchers. More than a million people have responded enthusiastically to PsychAlive and have expressed gratitude for the information it continues to provide. When one of Robert's articles for PsychAlive (Firestone 2013a) also appeared as a post on his *The Human Experience* blog (Firestone 2013b), we decided that the article's subject matter would make an interesting book for the general public. The result of our collaboration is the book you are holding in your hands.

What to Expect from This Book

This book will push you to take a hard look at your internal barriers to love, and at your fear of getting free of them. All ten chapters include constructive suggestions for countering your defenses. The first three chapters introduce fundamental information that lays the groundwork for the subjects covered later on. The next six chapters prompt you to examine your reactions when specific defenses are threatened by love. The last chapter offers some final advice that will help you maintain a loving relationship going forward.

Chapter 1 discusses how we get in our own way when we want to have love in our lives, and it goes on to explain how defenses create psychological barriers to love.

Chapter 2 exposes a destructive internal process—the critical inner voice—that supports our defenses and acts to undermine our intimate relationships.

Chapter 3 presents a method, based on Robert's technique of Voice Therapy, for challenging the critical inner voice and overcoming the psychological defenses that interfere with love.

Chapter 4 describes how we defend ourselves when love makes us feel vulnerable, and it offers suggestions for sustaining vulnerability.

Chapter 5 discusses how love interferes with a core defense—the fantasy bond, a defense that involves forming an imaginary connection with another person, and that often replaces genuine love in a romantic relationship. It presents actions that you can take to challenge your fantasy bond and keep love alive in your relationship.

Chapter 6 explores how we are conflicted when our positive feelings from love contradict our negative identity from childhood. It also offers a path to your being able to reject your old identity and instead accept the new one.

Chapter 7 discusses how the happiness we feel from love can leave us feeling guilty in relation to someone significant to us who is lonely or unhappy. It describes how to address these various guilty reactions.

Chapter 8 describes how we tend to defend ourselves when love and intimacy arouse sadness in us. It examines our fear of sadness and reveals the benefits of being open to feeling it.

Chapter 9 explains how we push love away when love and emotional attachment evoke our fears of loss and our awareness of death. It also explains how facing these existential realities can, in fact, enrich your life and make your relationships more meaningful.

Chapter 10 concludes the book with advice that will help you preserve your individuality, develop your communication skills, deal with anger constructively, and engage in the act of loving.

Another major element of using this book is journaling. Every chapter includes journal exercises that enable you to take the provocative information you are learning and make it personal by applying it to yourself and your relationship. The exercises also show you how to identify the behavior that keeps you defended, and how to challenge the critical inner voice that supports that behavior. There are exercises that assist you in planning and taking action to confront your defenses and sustain your romantic relationship. Specific exercises support your vulnerability and your positive identity. Others help you recognize and resist the formation of a fantasy bond in your relationship. Still others show you how to deal with guilt, accept sadness, and maintain intimacy in spite of the possibility of loss and the reality of death. In other words, the journal exercises, through direct and straightforward questions and prompts that help you investigate how and why you push love away, will stimulate you to engage in a deep and demanding process of personal discovery.

If you prefer the traditional handwritten approach, you will need to get a journal before you start chapter 1. Or you can go with a digital format, using a Word document, an online journaling platform, journaling software, or a journaling app for your iPhone, iPad, or Android device. Either method, handwritten or digital, is fine; choose the one that is more convenient for you and that you feel more comfortable using.

And Here We Go ...

During the self-reflective process that will be stimulated and guided by this book, it is essential that you maintain an attitude of compassion and sympathetic concern toward yourself, just as you would for a friend who was struggling. Be curious and accepting, not judgmental or condemning. With compassion for yourself, you can develop an understanding of what limits you in your intimate relationship. You will benefit as you come to see yourself and your partner from an interested and caring perspective rather than through the eyes of your inner critic. Accepting that you are human, and realizing that change takes time, will allow you to have a kind attitude toward yourself as you strive to allow more love into your life.

This book deals with a very unpleasant reality—when it comes to sabotaging love, we are our own biggest problem. But the book also carries an optimistic message—we are our only real solution to this problem. The act of looking within, to identify the defenses that obstruct love and then learn how to challenge them, is the very thing that provides a way to establish or recapture the feelings of friendship and love that we desire in our intimate relationship.

We cannot affect external influences like the passage of time or the unusual circumstances that can present themselves in life, and we can't really change other people. The only actual power we have in a relationship is that of developing ourselves. Therefore, our greatest task when it comes to sustaining love is that of increasing our capacity for intimacy and closeness.

There's a saying: "Once you have learned to love, you have learned to live." Let's begin that lesson.

CHAPTER 1

Our Defenses and How They Get in the Way of Love

When you open yourself to the continually changing, impermanent, dynamic nature of your own being and of reality, you increase your capacity to love and care about other people and your capacity to not be afraid.... You begin to think of your life as offering endless opportunities to start to do things differently.

—Pema Chödrön, *Practicing Peace in Times of War*

We all say that we want to find love. And most of us imagine that finding it is probably the biggest hurdle we'll face, as far as love goes. But the truth is that the primary obstacle to love is within us. Our biggest challenge isn't finding love; it's confronting our defenses against it and daring to allow love to develop.

Of course, most of us don't see it that way. We see love as eluding us. When we reflect on our relationships that have failed, we tend to think of mysterious external elements as the problem: "We grew apart." "He didn't try anymore." "She never let anything go." "We just weren't right for each other." We even go so far as to blame love itself: "True love doesn't last." "Marriage kills romance." "The spark always fades."

Despite our natural desire for kindness, affection, respectful treatment, romance, sex, and companionship, our long-established system of defenses, which was once necessary, now cuts us off from experiencing the life force that is love. This chapter examines how our defenses, even though they're outdated and irrelevant, continue to influence us to react against something that not only feels good but is also something that we innately desire as human beings. The chapter's journal exercises will help you identify defenses and an attachment pattern from your childhood, as well as defenses and an attachment style that are limiting you in your life today, especially in your romantic relationship.

What Is Love?

Why do we turn away from an experience that enhances our lives and gives such profound meaning to our existence? How can we reject what is probably the strongest and most personal expression of ourselves? To understand this paradox, it is important for us to establish what love is, since love is not only the subject of this book but also what most of us desire to have and maintain.

But love is tricky to define. In fact, for a number of years, the most searched question on Google has been "What is love?" (*Daily Mail* 2014). In addition, the words that are used to describe love have lost much of their original meaning. Many have become clichés; even those that depict the subtleties of love have been exploited and trivialized through manipulation and overuse. Advertising campaigns, the media, television shows, and movies have all done their part to dilute these words' meanings.

Love is not just a noun; perhaps more important, it is also a verb. But we often treat love as if it were only a noun. The state of being in love is passive and can easily become an internal fantasy about being loving. In contrast, the act of loving involves specific kinds of behaviors that keep a person dynamically engaged in love's expression.

What Interferes with Love?

Defenses, in a word, are what most interfere with love. By definition, defenses are a means or method of protecting ourselves (R. W. Firestone 1997a; Gilbert 1989). Our psychological defenses are strategies that we devise on a subconscious level to cope with anxiety and painful experiences. Most are formed in early childhood, in response to pain caused by deprivation, rejection, and fear of separation. Although these defenses were necessary when we were young and at the mercy of our environment, they are no longer appropriate to us as striving, active adults who can control our world, to a large extent. Unfortunately, however, fear of change often causes us to cling to our defenses; it restricts us in our lives and limits us in our most important relationships.

Our defenses are the reason why we or our partner (or both of us) may attempt to withdraw to what we feel is a safer distance after a particularly close moment in our relationship. But because this aversive reaction to love is largely unconscious, we often fail to identify the underlying defenses that are causing us to react in this way. We try to make sense of our rejecting or hostile behavior by attributing it to circumstances or blaming it on others, particularly our loved ones. Consider the example of Meredith:

> Meredith was divorced and living as a single mother. She had a lot on her plate. With her full-time job and a son with a learning disability, she had little time to even think about dating. She couldn't imagine finding a man who would have much interest in sharing such a difficult life with her.
>
> But Meredith got lucky. On a lark, she let a friend sign her up on an internet dating site, and when Daniel reached out to her, they began dating.
>
> Daniel was an easygoing guy, not the kind of person who made a lot of demands. If Meredith wasn't always available, that was fine with him. As they spent more time together, Daniel formed a strong relationship with her son, Justin. The boy responded to Daniel's warm personality and

sense of humor, and he welcomed Daniel's offers to help him with his schoolwork.

Meredith and Daniel had been together for more than a year when Daniel had the idea of taking her and Justin away for a weekend. As a surprise, he booked time at the spa for Meredith while he took Justin to the pool. The vacation was a success; all three of them had a good time together and returned home rested and happy. Meredith was touched by the experience and grateful for Daniel's thoughtfulness and sensitivity.

However, in the weeks that followed, Meredith became increasingly critical of Daniel. At first her comments were intermittent, and he was only slightly irritated by them. But over time, most of what she said to him was negative.

Daniel started to feel that he couldn't do anything right. He told a friend, "There is so much she's critical of about me, I don't even know why she wants to be with me anymore! It's like she hates me ever since that weekend we went away together."

How Defenses Are Formed

Numerous biological, environmental, and societal forces impact children during their early years and lead them to form defenses (R. W. Firestone 1985; Shapiro 2000). Children are affected by circumstantial influences, such as illness and poverty. They are also impacted by relational influences, such as rejection, frustration, and separation, which occur to some extent in every childhood. Defenses function to reduce a child's experience of emotional pain, anxiety, sadness, shame, and other overwhelming feelings. In cases of extreme trauma, defenses protect children in a situation that they perceive as life-threatening. Whatever the circumstances, defenses help children make the best adaptation they can.

Defenses from Early Childhood

The human child is born into an inherently flawed situation because the young child is totally reliant on his or her parents for physical and emotional survival over a prolonged period of time. According to neuroscientists, the development of an infant's mind is almost completely dependent on stimuli from the people in the immediate environment, especially during the first two years of life (Cozolino 2006; Schore 1994, 2003a, 2009; Siegel 1999; Siegel & Hartzell 2003). Unfortunately, it is not possible for even the best parents to be perfectly and completely attuned to their offspring. Therefore, there is no way, even under the best circumstances, that an infant's needs can be fully met.

Researchers have found that the defensive strategy a particular child adopts to cope with this dilemma is determined by multiple factors involving the individual disposition of that child, the psychological state of the parent or parents, and the environment the baby is born into (Briere 1992; Chess & Thomas 1986; Garbarino 1995; Meaney 2010; Perry 2002). Take, for example, Tina and Matilda, two sisters only a year apart, who developed very different personalities in the same family environment:

Tina and Matilda's mother suffered from postpartum depression during their infancy and continued to battle depression throughout their early childhood. Each girl devised different means of coping and getting her needs met. Tina, the older sister, was calmer by nature and responded to her mother's unavailability by withdrawing and self-soothing—for example, by sucking her thumb. Her younger sister, Matilda, was by nature more extroverted and reactive, and she responded by overtly demanding her mother's attention—for example, by throwing fits.

During later childhood, Tina and Matilda continued to operate much as they had when they were babies. Tina was quiet and shy, well behaved in school, and interested in solitary pursuits. Matilda was talkative and rambunctious; she was always acting up in class and was involved in many social activities. Tina withdrew from confrontation, whereas Matilda faced it head-on. Tina was sensitive and compassionate toward others, whereas Matilda could be headstrong and domineering.

Somewhere between two and six years of age, the child suffers a major trauma when she begins to become conscious of death (Hoffman & Strauss 1985; Kastenbaum 2000). Characters in stories die, a pet dies, and then at some point it occurs to her that her parents are going to die. The anticipated loss of her primary source of warmth, affection, and love evokes deep sadness, pain, and fear. Initially, the child does not realize that she faces the same fate, but eventually she comes to comprehend that she does. This has a traumatic effect: it destroys the child's illusion of immortality and permanence. The world that she believed to be never-ending is essentially turned upside down by the dawning comprehension that people, including her parents and herself, will die.

To deal with these new existential realities, children rely on the defenses they established earlier in childhood. They lean heavily on these defenses to relieve the fear, anger, sadness, disbelief, and confusion that threaten to overwhelm them. Eventually, they detach from their conscious awareness of death and drive it into their subconscious, and as they do so, they become even more dependent on their defenses to keep the fear and dread from resurfacing. And when they become adults, the same fear and dread will continue to be triggered when they experience fear of loss in their love relationships.

Defenses from Later Childhood

As children grow older, they continue to rely on the same defenses they developed in infancy. Their physical needs are no longer the same, but when their parents do not respond to their emotional needs, children feel the impact. And, according to researchers in neuroscience (Perry 2001; Schore 2003a), even before children are capable of talking about their experiences, the ways in which their parents interact (or fail to interact) with them have already become hardwired into children's brains.

When parents lack the ability to reflect on their own and their children's emotional states, they tend to behave, despite their best intentions, in ways that negatively affect their children. Parents' unwitting and unconscious behavior most often takes the form of such minor infractions as irritability, offhand criticism, or casual sarcasm. Hostility can also be communicated to a child through derisive, disapproving, or condescending commentary. Other, less noticeable forms of mistreatment include lack of respect for a child's personal boundaries, excessive permissiveness (which the child often perceives as indifference or neglect), overprotection, and emotional unavailability.

Sometimes parents lose their temper with their children and fly out of control. In these types of interactions, parents often manifest fierce, punitive attitudes or even violent rage, emotional reactions that stand out from their typical behavior. These dramatic reactions are frightening and confusing to a child. Children, partly because of their smaller size, can experience an angry or disciplinary encounter as dangerous and threatening. Even an incident that may seem relatively innocuous to an adult may be traumatic for a child. Moreover, the threatening nature of the experience is intensified by the child's reliance on the parent for love and care. During all of these types of interactions, children not only employ their old defenses but also develop new ones to cope with the problematic and sometimes frightening situation.

Journal Exercise 1.1. Childhood Defenses

This journal exercise will help you identify the defenses that you developed during your childhood. Consider the following prompts, and write your thoughts in your journal.

- Think about yourself as a child and the ways you coped with your emotions. For example, how did you react when you were hurt? When you were afraid? When you were angry? Did you lash out? Did you become anxious and agitated? Did you withdraw into your self? Did you sulk and pout?

- How did you act at times when you were frustrated and your needs weren't being met? Were you demanding? Did you throw a tantrum to get your way? Did you self-soothe to calm yourself? Did you adopt the attitude "I don't need anything from anyone"?

- Do you remember when you first became aware of death? Do you remember your reaction? Were you distressed? Have you blocked out the memory? How did the adults in your life respond to you then? Were they sympathetic and understanding of your feelings? Were they dismissive? Were they uncomfortable with the subject? Did they comfort you?

Childhood Attachment Patterns

Attachment theorists study the dynamics in long-term interpersonal relationships, including the relationships formed in early childhood and adulthood (Ainsworth 1989; Ainsworth, Blehar, Waters, & Wall 1978; Bowlby 1982, 1988; Main & Hesse 1990). There are two approaches to attachment that are somewhat independent. One studies the attachment patterns between infant and caregiver; the other studies the attachment style of partners in romantic relationships. Researchers who study childhood attachment have observed the different ways in which children go about establishing both emotional and physical attachments to their principal caregivers. The pattern of attachment that an individual child leans toward is primarily dependent on the qualities of the caregiving adult.

There are four main types of childhood attachment: secure, avoidant, anxious, and disorganized. All but the secure attachment style foster different defensive reactions and coping mechanisms.

A child develops secure attachment patterns when he has a parent or other significant adult who is, for the most part, sensitive and responsive during interactions with the child. This parent or other adult is attuned and available to the child in ways that make the child feel seen and safe. When the child is hurting, this adult treats him with compassion and offers comfort. Such an adult is a strong and consistent presence in the child's life, supporting the child's independence with a caring interest that is fortifying as the child goes forth into the world. The child with secure attachment patterns is well adjusted and develops fewer defenses. He is comfortable within himself and at ease in relating to others.

A child develops avoidant attachment patterns when she has a parent or other significant adult who is primarily unavailable and emotionally distant. This type of caregiving adult is preoccupied with his or her own life, largely unaware of the child, and often oblivious to or insensitive to her needs. When the child is hurting or distressed, this adult has little or no response to her. He or she often discourages the child from crying. The child becomes seemingly independent at a very young age, a "little adult" who doesn't need anything from anyone else, especially this adult. The child with avoidant attachment patterns develops the defense of being self-sufficient and wanting very little from others. She is self-contained, keeps to herself, and has minimal interactions with other people. Meredith, whom we met earlier, offers an example of someone who developed avoidant patterns of attachment during childhood:

> Meredith's mother had been sickly, and her father was
> preoccupied with tending to her, so Meredith had to grow up
> fast, and she quickly learned how to fend for herself. She felt
> that she was all alone in her family, especially when her
> mother was bedridden and Meredith had to tend to her.
> Meredith took care of herself and expected little from others.

A child develops anxious attachment patterns when he has a parent or other significant adult whose behavior is inconsistent and contradictory. At times this adult is responsive and nurturing, but at other times he or she can be intrusive and emotionally hungry or distant and emotionally unavailable. This leaves the child confused and insecure, never knowing what kind of treatment to expect from his caregiver. Typically, the child with anxious attachment patterns is clingy with his parent and acts desperate toward him or her. He tends to be distrustful and insecure. He is agitated and can't calm down or feel at peace. His defensive reaction is to cling to his parent in an effort to get his needs met.

A child develops disorganized attachment patterns if she has a parent or other significant adult who is physically and/or emotionally abusive toward her. At such times, the child often responds to this adult's frightening behavior by psychologically detaching from the experience. In a sense, she is no longer in her body, and afterward she has little or no memory of what occurred. The child with disorganized attachment patterns is torn between wanting and fearing her caregiver because her abuser and her source of comfort are in fact the same person. She runs up to her parent for safety, but as she gets close, she feels unsafe and pulls away. Her defensive solution is to escape this nightmarish dilemma by being emotionally disconnected.

Journal Exercise 1.2. Childhood Attachment Patterns

Identifying the patterns of attachment that you developed during your childhood can help you gain insight into the defenses that you developed when you were young. Consider the following prompts, and write your thoughts in your journal.

- As you were reading about the different types of attachment patterns, did a particular one resonate with you?

- Did one of the patterns seem to be describing you and your childhood experience?

- If so, can you recognize any defensive behavior that you developed along with your pattern of attachment?

Adult Attachment Styles

Our early defensive patterns continue throughout our lives, and they continue to limit us in adulthood, even though they become largely dysfunctional at some point and are no longer appropriate. But they are deeply ingrained in our psyches because the brain lays down strong memory traces of experiences that are frightening or are felt to be life-threatening (Baumeister, Bratslavsky, Finkenauer, & Vohs 2001; Vaish, Grossmann, & Woodward 2008). In other words, memory traces from early childhood sustain our defenses as adults, a process that colors our perceptions of the world and influences how we relate to others.

For example, if you were neglected as a child, you may have developed the defense of being inward and self-sufficient and not asking for anything from anyone else. This defense leaves you feeling cynical and distrustful of people and assuming that they will ignore or disregard you. If adults in your childhood were intrusive and disrespectful of your boundaries, you may shy away from close contact. You now keep others at a distance because you fear that you will be consumed if you get too close.

Attachment researchers who study adult romantic relationships have identified four primary styles of attachment in adult relationships: secure, dismissive avoidant, anxious preoccupied, and fearful avoidant (Mikulincer & Shaver 2016, especially chapter 2, "A Model of Attachment-System Functioning and Dynamics in Adulthood"). Our adult attachment styles—that is, the insecure styles—can be indicators of the childhood defenses that are continuing to affect us in our close relationships (Mikulincer & Shaver 2016).

Adults with a secure attachment style are more satisfied in their romantic relationships. Their relationships tend to be honest, open, and equal, with both partners being independent yet loving toward each other. There is little drama in these types of relationships. Adults with secure attachment patterns are less defended against intimacy and love.

Adults with a dismissive avoidant attachment style in their romantic relationships tend to seek isolation and feel pseudoindependent, their primary focus being self-sufficiency. They can't acknowledge their own needs or those of others, and are therefore dismissing and disregarding of their partner's needs. They are more comfortable with casual encounters and short-term relationships. In a more personal relationship, their defensive reaction is to emotionally distance themselves from their partner. They deny the importance of loved ones, and they detach from them easily.

Meredith's dismissive avoidant attachment style persisted in her adult life. Although generally independent and self-sufficient, in her relationships she often acted as a caregiver, much as she had with her mother. She married a man who couldn't hold down a job, and eventually abandoned her. She was also financially responsible for their son. Sometimes she was overwhelmed by her circumstances, but it never occurred to her to ask for help. Before she met Daniel, she had become cynical about ever finding love.

Adults with an anxious preoccupied attachment style in their romantic relationships tend to be insecure and unsure of their partner's feelings and feel unsafe in their close relationships. Their defensive reaction is to be clingy, demanding, or possessive toward their partner. They are frequently looking to their partner to rescue or complete them.

Adults with a fearful avoidant attachment style in their romantic relationships live in an ambivalent state, afraid of being too close to others but also afraid of being too distant. They are trapped in a defensive reaction to love: they go toward love, but when they get close to someone, they pull away for fear that they will be hurt. They may cling to their partner when they feel rejected, and then they may feel trapped when the partner gets close. They are often unpredictable in their moods. They try to keep a lid on their feelings but are often overwhelmed by their emotions. Their close relationships tend to be rocky or dramatic, with many highs and lows. Adults with a fearful avoidant attachment style are often in turbulent relationships.

Journal Exercise 1.3. Adult Attachment Styles

Identifying your particular style of attachment can help you gain insight into the defenses that are limiting you in your personal relationships today. Consider the following prompts, and write your thoughts in your journal.

- As you were reading about the different types of adult attachment styles, did a particular one resonate with you?

- Did one of the styles seem to be describing you and how you feel today?

- If so, can you identify any defensive behavior that corresponds to your style of attachment in your romantic relationships?

Even though our defenses operate outside our conscious awareness, we react when they are threatened. For example, being chosen and especially valued brings happiness and fulfillment, but if that interferes with our old self-protective habits, we push love away. We are averse to upsetting our psychological equilibrium by disrupting our established defenses. Our defensive adaptation compels us to continue viewing ourselves, others, and the world around us the way we did as children.

Daniel's acts of love and kindness threatened Meredith's primary defense—taking care of herself and never wanting anything from anyone. Daniel challenged Meredith's dismissive avoidant style of relating. But Meredith was learning to trust Daniel and accept what he offered her and Justin. On their weekend away, she was especially happy and touched by his generosity.

Afterward, however, without being aware of it, Meredith began to feel anxious from how undefended and vulnerable she had been with Daniel. She noticed that she had become irritable and critical toward him, but she didn't know why. She thought that maybe she was stressed at work.

After Daniel talked with his friend, he spoke to Meredith about the change in her behavior toward him. They traced it back to their romantic weekend, and Meredith realized that she'd become afraid after being so open to Daniel and exposing herself to the possibility of being hurt in their relationship.

Meredith's relationship with Daniel is reshaping her style of attachment. With Daniel, she is gradually relinquishing her dismissive avoidant attachment style and forming a new, secure style of attachment.

Should we let our defenses go and trust in love? Or should we hold on to our self-protective approach to life and push a loved one away? Giving up defenses that we once felt to be lifesaving can feel very threatening, and it's a tough choice. But the choice is also obvious.

Summary and a Look Ahead

As children, we had to develop methods for protecting ourselves psychologically when we were in emotional pain. We were at the mercy of our environment—passive victims who had to adapt to situations we could not change. But an adaptation that begins as a constructive way of coping becomes an imprisoning agent because once a defense is in place, it's hard to believe we can live without it. A defense is very much like scar tissue from a burn—the scar originally protected us from further damage, but now it only disfigures us. And yet there's good reason for optimism. When we become aware of our defenses, and when we understand how they limit us, we can take action to break the defensive habits that are interfering with love. And then we're in a position to understand and challenge the critical inner voice, a destructive process that drives our defenses and forms the topic of the next chapter.

CHAPTER 2

The Critical Inner Voice That Supports Our Defenses

We get seduced by our own mantras (*I'm a failure … I'm lonely … I'm a failure … I'm lonely …*) and we become monuments to them.

—Elizabeth Gilbert, *Eat, Pray, Love*

To varying degrees, we all have an enemy within, a part of ourselves that operates inside our heads in much the same way a malicious coach does, criticizing us and offering up bad advice. This enemy, with its angry point of view, is our *critical inner voice* (R. W. Firestone 1987, 1997a, 1997b). It speaks the malicious language of our defenses, and what it supports is not our loving, vulnerable selves but our destructive behavior and attitudes. It comments negatively on our lives and condemns our actions. It picks us apart and destroys our confidence and self-esteem. And it undermines our romantic relationships by criticizing those we love and running us down for loving them (R. W. Firestone, Firestone, & Catlett 2002). This chapter discusses that critical voice within us and explains how it operates. The chapter's journal exercises will show you how to identify your own critical inner voice that attacks you, your partner, and your relationship.

Your Real Self and the Anti-Self

We are all aware of having mixed feelings toward ourselves and, at times, of being self-critical. Our mixed feelings and self-criticisms represent a split within us that has been conceptualized as a "division of the mind" between forces that support our "real self" and opposing forces that support the "anti-self" (R. W. Firestone 1997b, 37–42). For the most part, we're unaware of this split, and of the destructive impact it has on our lives.

Your real self consists of your unique characteristics. They include your biological, temperamental, and genetic traits; your identification with the positive qualities and behavior of your parents and other caring adults; and the beneficial effects of your upbringing, education, and ongoing experience. Your positive traits and constructive attitudes are harmoniously assimilated into your real self.

The anti-self, an alien part of your personality, makes its presence known when your critical inner voice attacks you and others in your life. The anti-self is an accumulation of the destructive attitudes and defenses you developed during your formative years. It also includes certain self-soothing strategies, such as addictions, that are contrary to your best interests. The defensive attitudes of the anti-self, unlike your positive traits and constructive attitudes, cannot be integrated into your real self because they oppose it, and this is what creates the division within the mind.

Let's begin to take a closer look at this inner dynamic by considering the example of Kevin:

> Kevin met Haley while she was in her last year of college. Before dating her, he had enjoyed the single life, but now he wanted a more serious relationship. By the end of the school year, they had become very close.
>
> After Haley graduated, she went away for a monthlong vacation, and Kevin missed her so much that when she returned, he asked her to live with him. Haley was torn between her original plan of moving back to her hometown and the idea of sharing her life with Kevin. She eventually

chose to move home, even though Kevin tried to convince her to stay. But after three months, she decided to go back and move in with Kevin, and he was thrilled.

After a short time, however, Kevin began to feel stifled living with Haley. He found excuses for not coming home, and when he was home, he was uncommunicative and unaffectionate.

He could see that his behavior was hurting Haley, and he wondered why he was suddenly having these negative reactions. After all, Haley was the same person she had been before. And Kevin had been so desperate for them to live together! But now he felt that he was suffocating.

How the Critical Inner Voice Develops

The critical inner voice—the language of the anti-self—develops early in childhood, at the same time that stressful circumstances cause children to form defenses. In the process, children also form negative views of themselves as they assimilate negative attitudes or feelings directed toward them, taking these on as their own point of view toward themselves.

And it isn't even necessary to convey negative or critical words directly to a child—children pick up on parents' and other caregivers' underlying anger and hostility, and they integrate these feelings in the form of attacks by the critical inner voice. For example, if a child is suffering from rejection, she often takes on a critical inner voice that tells her that she is too needy. A child who is left sad and hurting may develop an inner voice that tells him that he is too fussy. If a child is made to feel angry and frustrated, the inner voice often tells her that she is unruly and out of control, and if she is punished, the inner voice tells her that she deserves punishment.

This critical inner voice remains intact beyond childhood and continues to shape people's lives. The inner voice that once told a child she was too needy now advises her, as an adult, not to burden others with her wants. The inner voice that said a child was too fussy now tells the adult he has become not to show his emotions. The inner voice that accused a child of being unruly comes down on her in adulthood whenever she feels a trace of anger. The inner voice that told a child he deserved punishment continues to tell him that he deserves to be treated badly as an adult.

And so the critical inner voice becomes the agent of a downward-spiraling process. As people persist in believing the voice's pronouncements—*You're an idiot! You're just not smart* or *You're so clumsy. You break everything!*—they act on these statements. Listening to these particular attacks, a person can grow more muddled in his thinking or find that she has become physically awkward and uncoordinated. That's because, over time, critical self-attacks predispose negative behavior, which then comes to form part of a person's style or approach to life. When we listen to the critical inner voice, accept what it says, and habitually believe it, we run the risk of becoming what that voice tells us we are.

How the Critical Inner Voice Operates

As we've seen, the critical inner voice is, in effect, the language of the anti-self. This voice works against your personal development, opposing your best interests and diminishing your sense of self. It is not your real point of view, which reflects your natural wants, your aspirations, and your desire for affiliation with others as well as your drive to be sexual, reproduce, and be creative. Rather, this voice represents a point of view that is alien to your real self and promotes self-limitation, self-destruction, and animosity toward other people. Its hostile, judgmental attitudes create a negative, pessimistic picture of the world you live in.

The critical inner voice exists in everyone, to some degree. It generally operates below the level of consciousness, so you don't experience it as a hallucination or an audible sound. However, you can identify it and discern its words, especially in stressful situations, when you're probably more aware of attacking yourself. When you make a mistake, you hear *Can't you ever do anything right?* Or when you venture outside your comfort zone—say, by agreeing to make a public presentation—you're likely to hear *You're going to mess up this speech and humiliate yourself in front of all these people!*

Pretending to Be Your Conscience

The critical inner voice represents your anti-self, not your conscience or values. The easiest way to distinguish this inner voice from your conscience is to recognize its punishing, degrading quality. Even when what it says appears to reflect a value system, its tone is often demeaning and vindictive, or coddling and indulgent. Instead of inspiring you to maintain an attitude of self-compassion and motivating you to take constructive action, the critical inner voice increases your self-hatred with categorical attacks that imply that you will never change. It engenders hopelessness about sustaining self-control and improving your life.

This voice has no integrity. It does not represent a consistent point of view; it plays both sides of an issue. It often instigates self-destructive actions and then condemns you when you take those actions. It encourages you to have that one drink too many or that extra helping of food and then criticizes your lack of willpower.

The critical inner voice does not represent a moral point of view. For example, it may condone and encourage self-denial: *When someone asks what you want for your birthday, do them a favor and tell them, "Nothing"* or *It's a waste of money to go on vacation.* That kind of self-sacrificing behavior is hurtful, both to the person who engages in it and to others. When you refuse a gift, you prevent someone from expressing loving feelings toward you in this particular way, and from experiencing the gratification that comes from giving. If you deny yourself a vacation, you deprive yourself, your friends, and your family of spending relaxing and recreational time with you. Indeed, although self-sacrifice may masquerade as a value, it is not at all humanitarian, because it supports any tendency you may have to give up your wants and needs, which means, in effect, giving up significant parts of your identity.

Attacking Your Real Self

The critical inner voice can also be conceived of as a filter that alters what you hear about yourself, others, and present-day events. When your thoughts are distorted by this filter, your perceptions of your current life are inaccurate. Even in its mildest forms, this voice inhibits your ability to pursue what you really want in life and to develop a true sense of who you are.

Sometimes the voice quashes your enthusiasm, excitement, and spontaneity: *Be quiet! No one wants to hear from you* or *Don't get so excited—you're making a fool of yourself* or *You're just trying to get attention.*

Sometimes it feeds your insecurity, urging you to withdraw from others and isolate yourself: *You are basically unlovable—just stay in the background* or *You don't matter, so don't bother other people with your problems* or *You're shy, so avoid socializing—you'll just embarrass yourself.*

It may make you feel undesirable, causing you to resist entering into a relationship, or interfering with your ability to deepen a relationship you're already in: *You are so ugly—no one would ever be attracted to you* or *You aren't any good in close relationships, so don't even bother trying* or *You aren't the kind of person someone would want to have children with.*

Or it may discourage you from wanting anything at all: *You're stupid to go after that job* or *Why go out tonight? Just stay home and watch TV* or *You're too old to be looking for love.*

Whenever you heed a critical inner voice that encourages you to give up your interest in and excitement about life—to stop participating in sports and other physical activities before you have to, or settle for diminished interest in sex and reduced sexual activity, or lose contact with old friends, or tolerate a declining social life—you constrict your life and put limits on your experiences. Unfortunately, though, the voice that promotes self-denial often finds support in society, especially when it comes to what is considered a gender-appropriate or age-appropriate role or behavior. Kevin gradually discovered this truth:

As Kevin struggled with his negative reactions to living with Haley, he began to become aware of an inner voice that was attacking him in his relationship: *What are you doing, tying yourself down with this woman? Don't you miss your single life? Don't you miss the fun you had? You're too restless to be happy with one woman. You're going to suffocate in this relationship. Get out!*

Journal Exercise 2.1. Identify How Your Critical Inner Voice Attacks Your Real Self

Read the following prompts, and record your thoughts in your journal.

- Think about a self-attack or self-criticism you often experience in a close relationship.

- Just pick one. It can be a small self-attack, like "I'm not a romantic person." Write that self-attack down, but change "I" to "you": *You're not a romantic person.*

- Now take some time to expand on that attack, continuing to use "you" instead of "I," and see where that takes you in your thinking. For example, the attacking thought *You're not romantic* may become *You're not the kind of person someone would feel romantic toward* and then *You're just not lovable!*

- Write down all these attacks by your critical inner voice.

Assuming a Soothing or Coddling Tone

Sometimes the critical inner voice seems to be protecting you and sounds as if it is acting in your best interests: *Why work so hard? You're only going to overexert yourself* or *Don't bother exercising today—just take a nap* or *Don't go out of town this summer—all that planning and packing is such a bother.* Regardless of its enticing tone, the voice expresses a destructive point of view and promotes destructive actions. In truth, this voice has the familiar sound of an overprotective parent who cautions, directs, controls, and advises you but whose purpose is really to squelch your enthusiasm, spontaneity, and sense of adventure.

Sometimes the voice takes on a soothing tone and may counsel you to isolate yourself: *You need your time alone* or *How can you stand being around these people all the time?* or *You'll feel better if you just go off by yourself for a while.* What the voice is saying may sound reasonable at first; obviously, you need some time alone for creative or concentrated work and for a break from the stresses of daily living. But extended periods of isolation from social contact are detrimental to mental health (Gove & Hughes 1980; Heckler 1994; Seiden 1984). The longer you isolate yourself, the stronger and more intense the attacks by your critical inner voice become. In fact, those attacks flourish in isolation, which is like a greenhouse for your critical inner voice, as Kevin began to suspect:

> Kevin recognized that his inner voice was encouraging him to be alone: *You're stuck with this woman 24/7. You never have time to yourself. You like being alone. You've got to get more time by yourself.*

Journal Exercise 2.2. Identify the Critical Inner Voice's Soothing or Coddling Tone

Read the following prompts, and record your thoughts in your journal.

- Think about thoughts you've had that were soothing or coddling and encouraged you to withdraw into yourself.

- Pick one example. Maybe you had a seemingly innocent thought, like "It's been a hard week. I just want to stay home and binge-watch my favorite show this weekend." Record that thought, but change "I" to "you": *After the week you've had, you deserve to hole up by yourself.*

- Now take some time to expand on that thought, continuing to use "you" instead of "I," and see where that takes you in your thinking. For example, the thought "I just want to close my door to the world, get a bottle of wine, and order some good take-out" may become *This will be fun—you know how to relax and have a good time* and then *You really don't need anyone else.*

- Write down all these soothing, coddling thoughts that come from your critical inner voice.

Encouraging Grandiosity

At other times, your critical inner voice appears to be acting in your best interests when it builds you up with exaggerated statements of praise: *You are amazing* or *You'll do a brilliant job on this assignment* or *You'll be the most beautiful person at the party* or *You're so smart—you're going to be at the absolute top of your class.* Such proclamations set the stage for a brutal attack from the critical inner voice when you inevitably fail to live up to them: *You are such a loser* or *You are a fraud* or *You are worthless.* Grandiose attitudes have nothing to do with feelings of self-regard or self-worth, or with a genuine appraisal of your abilities.

Journal Exercise 2.3. Identify How the Critical Inner Voice Encourages Grandiosity

Read the following prompts, and record your thoughts in your journal.

- Think about thoughts you've had that built you up with exaggerated praise and promoted grandiosity and vanity in you.

- Pick one example. Maybe you had a seemingly positive thought, like "I'm such a loving, giving person." Record that thought, but change it into a "you" statement: *You're such a loving, giving person.*

- Now take some time to expand on that thought, continuing to use "you" instead of "I," and see where that takes you in your thinking. For example, *You're such a loving, giving person* may become *None of the guys you've been with appreciated that about you* and then *The problem was that you were too good for them.*

- Write down all these statements from your critical inner voice.

Attacking Your Partner

Just as you have a split view of yourself, you also possess a split view of those who are significant to you. For example, at times you see your partner as lovable, and you have compassionate, affectionate feelings toward him or her. At other times you focus on your partner's faults and think of your partner in unfavorable, cynical terms. These contradictory views of your partner are yet another indication of the deep division within you. Kevin, too, found himself thinking about Haley in negative, cynical ways:

When Kevin explored what his critical inner voice had to say about Haley, he finally began to understand his avoidant reactions to living with her. He was listening to his inner voice telling him, *Are you sure she's The One? She doesn't seem that great. You can do much better.*

Journal Exercise 2.4. Identify How the Critical Inner Voice Attacks Your Partner

Read the following prompts, and record your thoughts in your journal.

- Think about an ongoing attack or criticism that you direct toward your partner.

- Just pick one. It could be a small attack or criticism, like "She is not considerate of me."

- Record that thought, but change "me" to "you," as if both of you were being talked about: *She isn't considerate of you.*

- Now take some time to expand on that thought, continuing to change "me" to "you," and see where that takes you in your thinking. *She's inconsiderate and doesn't care about you* may become *All she cares about is herself* and then *You don't mean anything to her.*

- Write down all these attacks and criticisms from your inner voice.

Attacking Your Relationship

The critical inner voice is not content with attacking you and your partner. It attacks your relationship, too: *You're acting ridiculous, like a couple of love-struck teenagers* or *You're both losers—let's see which one of you ruins this relationship* or *This relationship is never going to last.* Let's check back in with Kevin:

Kevin also caught his critical inner voice in the act of attacking his relationship: *You're both too young for a serious relationship. You're a couple of kids who don't know the first thing about love.*

Journal Exercise 2.5. Identify How the Critical Inner Voice Attacks Your Relationship

Read the following prompts, and record your thoughts in your journal.

- Consider a doubt or a critical thought that you have about your relationship.

- Just pick one. It could be a thought that doesn't appear to be negative, like "We really need to focus on keeping to our budget."

- Record that thought, but change "we" and "our" to "you" and "your," as if you were both being talked to: *You both need to pay more attention to your finances.*

- Now take some time to expand on this thought, continuing to change "we" and "our" to "you" and "your," and see where that takes you in your thinking. *You guys can't manage anything* may become *The two of you are so irresponsible and immature—you are like a couple of children* and then *There's no way this relationship can succeed.*

- Write down all these attacks by your critical inner voice.

Attacking People and Relationships in General

You're also affected by the generalizations that your critical inner voice is eager to share on the topics of people and relationships: *You can't trust anybody* or *No one really cares—everyone's looking out for number one* or *People are fundamentally dishonest—it's just human nature.* This voice generalizes about men and women, too: *Men don't have feelings—all they care about is sex* or *Women are irrational and overemotional* or *Women have less interest in sex than men do.* Kevin's critical inner voice had more than a few general remarks to offer about relationships:

> When Kevin listened for what his inner voice was telling him about relationships, this is what he heard: *Let me tell you what it's all about. All women want is to tie a guy down. They just want to possess you and keep you on a short leash. You're doomed. Get out while you can!*

Journal Exercise 2.6. Identify How Your Critical Inner Voice Attacks People and Relationships in General

Read the following prompts, and record your thoughts in your journal.

- Consider a doubt or a critical thought you have about people or relationships.

- Just pick one. It could be a generalization, like "Relationships never last." Record that thought, but add *You have to realize that …*, as if you were being talked to: *You have to realize that relationships never last.*

- Now take some time to expand on that thought, continuing to change it around so you are the one addressed, and see where that takes you in your thinking. *Look at all the couples you know—they're always breaking up* could become *Look at yourself! Your romantic relationships always end in failure* and then *It's stupid to even bother looking for love.*

- Write down all these generalizations from your critical inner voice.

Your critical inner voice's attacks on others usually coexist with its denigration of you. Both types of attacks support the views of your anti-self. For example, attacks like *You're unlovable* and *Those people don't want to be friends with you* promote a self-hating identity. The voice denigrating you (*You're so pathetic, you'll settle for anyone who comes along*) also denigrates your partner (*You deserve better than her*). Both attacks work toward the same end—destroying the possibility of your having an intimate relationship.

As Kevin became aware of the different types of attacks coming from his critical inner voice, he began to understand the extent of the internal process that was so intent on sabotaging his relationship with Haley. He could see how it was affecting his feelings and influencing him to reject her. With this clarity, Kevin could choose not to act on the advice of his critical inner voice. He could choose instead to take actions that supported his relationship with Haley—and represented his real self.

Summary and a Look Ahead

Our critical inner voice—our enemy within—causes much of our unnecessary pain and frustration. It influences us to turn away from our true motives and wants. Its warnings interfere with our self-expression and diminish our sense of identity. And when this voice invades the intimate space of our romantic relationship, it becomes the primary obstacle to closeness as it weakens our sense of self and erodes the love and equality between us and our partner, to the point where the companionship and sexual attraction we originally enjoyed are diminished or even lost. Until we can identify this critical inner voice, it's difficult or impossible for us to distinguish our real wants and desires from the destructive goals that this voice prescribes. But we can interrupt and reverse this destructive pattern when we learn how to confront and challenge the critical inner voice and its distortions about ourselves, our partner, and our relationship. The next chapter presents a method for doing just that.

CHAPTER 3

The Voice Therapy Method

Instead of thinking that I was a failure, could I perhaps accept that I am only a human being—and a normal one, at that?

—Elizabeth Gilbert, *Eat, Pray, Love*

How do we change the behavior and attitudes that are causing us to sabotage love? How can we stop attacking ourselves and accept that we are human beings worthy of love?

The first two chapters discussed why we push love away. They explained how our reactions result from thought processes and behavior that we developed in childhood, and that remain part of our identity and personality today.

This chapter outlines the Voice Therapy method, a six-step plan of action that is effective in bringing about change, and the chapter's journal exercises will help you apply the Voice Therapy method so you can challenge the critical inner voice that attacks you, your partner, and your relationship. It's hard work, and it takes commitment. But if you persevere, you will gain control over the behavior and attitudes that are damaging your relationship, and you'll be better able to maintain love and intimacy in your life.

Old Habits—and New Hope for Change

Our well-established ways of being are stubborn, entrenched in our psyches. They have been hardwired in our brains for a very long time. However, there is good news. Recent findings in neuroscience and psychology have shown that real change can occur.

Up until the 1960s, it was believed that the brain developed during infancy and childhood, and that by early adulthood its physical structure was permanent. But modern research has found that this is not true (Doidge 2007; Siegel 1999). For example, researchers in neuroscience have discovered that the brain continues to develop and adjust throughout a person's lifetime (Doidge 2007). According to B. Kolb, Robbin, & Robinson (2003, 1), "Although the brain was once seen as a rather static organ, it is now clear that the organization of brain circuitry is constantly changing as a function of experience." This newly discovered ability, called "brain plasticity" or "neuroplasticity," is also known as "cortical remapping," a term that refers to the fact that the brain continues to create new neural pathways and alter existing ones as it adapts to new experiences, learns new information, and creates new memories (Lane, Ryan, Nadel, & Greenberg 2015). In addition, behavioral researchers have identified the factors necessary for bringing about change (Cozolino 2015). These involve preparation, planning, action, and maintenance (Lickerman 2012). The six steps of Voice Therapy correspond to these change factors.

All of this is not to say that change is easy, however. When it comes to altering old patterns that sabotage love, it takes much more than an encouraging slogan like Nike's "Just do it" or Oprah Winfrey's "Live your best life." To change, you cannot rely only on resolve and good intentions. To make a real difference, your approach has to be pragmatic. And that's where Voice Therapy comes in.

The Voice Therapy Method

This method is called Voice Therapy because it is literally a process of voicing—of giving spoken words to—the negative thought patterns that govern our self-limiting, self-destructive behavior. Its six steps help us effectively identify the enemy within—the anti-self, with its critical inner voice—that undermines our efforts to establish a loving relationship. When we bring this enemy out of hiding and into the open, we can challenge it. That's because its tactics and attitudes become clear to us when they're exposed in this way, and this clarity makes it easier for us to formulate a plan for overcoming the influence of the anti-self. As we saw in chapter 2, when your critical inner voice attacks your love relationship, it attacks on three different flanks— you, your loved one, and the relationship between you. You can use the six steps of Voice Therapy to counter each of these assaults.

Later in the chapter, you will learn how to use the Voice Therapy method to confront your critical inner voice as it attacks you, your partner, and your relationship. For now, meet Gloria and Nick:

> Gloria and Nick had been married for six years. Early in their marriage, Gloria pursued her career, but when their two children were born, she chose to stay home to raise them.
>
> Eventually Nick got a promotion at work, and he began putting in extra hours to learn his new tasks and responsibilities. He often came home late at night, and he worked on many weekends. He missed spending time with Gloria and their children, and he looked forward to settling into his job and getting his life back.
>
> Gloria missed Nick, too. Even before his promotion, she had been struggling with feelings of loneliness and isolation. During long hours of being alone or spending time only with their young children, she had been experiencing self-critical thoughts that she hadn't had in years, attacks that fueled her insecurity and left her feeling depressed and hopeless. For example, she had put on a little weight after the birth of the second baby, and now she was critical of her body. She feared that Nick was losing interest in her and that he wasn't as attracted to her as before. She even worried that he might want to leave her. She reacted to his absences as if they were personal rejections, and as she became more self-hating and

insecure in relation to Nick, Gloria withdrew from him. But when Nick grew worried about her depressed mood, he encouraged Gloria to talk to someone, and she sought professional help.

Throughout the rest of this section, we'll see how Gloria, working with her therapist, learned to apply the six steps of Voice Therapy.

Step 1. Identify

Step 1 of the Voice Therapy method is to *identify* your critical thoughts about yourself, your partner, and your relationship. Your critical inner voice often runs a covert operation, belittling you, your partner, and your relationship on what is basically a subliminal level. Its attitudes and criticisms have been with you for so long that you probably experience them as a faint droning noise or a nagging worry at the back of your mind, a disturbance you barely notice.

How can you become aware of what your critical inner voice is telling you? Think first about the ways in which you criticize *yourself*. How are you hard on yourself? How do you compare yourself unfavorably to others? What are the critical thoughts that you imagine other people have toward you?

> Gloria's negative thoughts took the form of "I'm not interesting anymore. I'm not the same person I was when I was working. I'm not fun to be with anymore. I'm not attractive."

If you have trouble accessing negative thoughts about yourself, try thinking about a behavior of yours that may be inhibiting intimacy with your partner. For example, you may be using a particular substance (alcohol, drugs, food) or a habitual activity (video gaming, TV watching, exercising) in an addictive or compulsive way. If so, your use of this substance or activity is most likely serving to suppress your thoughts and feelings. Try dropping this substance or activity for a time, and pay attention to the thoughts and feelings that begin to arise.

Gloria realized that she was using food to soothe herself when she felt bad or lonely. She decided to stop overeating and then see how she felt. This decision left her anxious but also more aware of her negative thoughts about herself: "Who am I kidding? I'm fat. I'm not attractive anymore. I'm past my prime. I'm just a chubby, matronly mom."

Now think about the ways in which you are critical of *your partner*. What are your cynical thoughts about him or her? What disparaging comments do you make about your partner? What are your angry fantasies about him or her?

Gloria's critical thoughts about Nick were "He doesn't care about me. He's at work all the time. He's not attracted to me anymore. It's like he doesn't want to be around me."

Finally, what are your negative thoughts about *your relationship*? What sarcastic remarks do you make about it? What are your skeptical attitudes about romance and love?

Gloria identified a number of negative thoughts about her relationship with Nick: "I'm the one who makes the effort in this relationship. I'm the one who puts the energy into it, the one who's invested in it. If it weren't for me, Nick would be happy for it to just die out. This is just what happens after a while."

Do you have negative thoughts like Gloria's? If so, they can help you identify how your critical inner voice is attacking you, your partner, your relationship, and love in general. You may feel nervous or anxious as you become more fully aware of such thoughts. That's because these thoughts are directly tied to well-established defenses that are no longer necessary in your adult life, but we are often afraid to change something that has been such an integral part of how we've always operated. And even though your negative thoughts and attitudes do not reflect your dominant feelings about your partner, you may still feel shaken when you identify them. If so, keep in mind that the purpose of exploring these types of thoughts is to discover the point of view of the inner, often hidden enemy that is working against you, your partner, and your relationship.

Step 2. Verbalize

Step 2 of the Voice Therapy method is to directly *verbalize* the attacks of your critical inner voice against you, your partner, and your relationship. You do this by returning to the thoughts that were "I" statements in step 1 and expressing them now as "you" statements. This step is at the heart of Voice Therapy. It is not meant to be rushed through, because it involves a process that can be intense and emotional. This step helps you become more aware of your critical inner voice on a conscious level.

Look at the critical thoughts about *yourself* that you became aware of in step 1. Now change those thoughts from "I" statements *about* yourself to "you" statements directed *toward* yourself. Here is what happened when Gloria performed step 2 of Voice Therapy:

> For Gloria, the thoughts "I'm not interesting anymore. I'm not the same person I was when I was working. I'm not fun to be with anymore. I'm not attractive" became *You're not interesting anymore. You're not the same person you were when you were working. You're not fun to be with anymore. You're not attractive.* And "Who am I kidding? I'm fat. I'm not attractive anymore. I'm past my prime. I'm just a chubby, matronly mom" became *Who are you kidding? You're fat. You're not attractive anymore. You're past your prime. You're just a chubby, matronly mom.*

Say these "you" statements out loud. As you do, pay attention to the feelings and thoughts that arise. When you express your self-critical thoughts as attacks by your critical inner voice, even angrier and meaner thoughts can arise and trigger an all-out attack.

> Gloria continued to change her "I" statements to "you" statements: *Nobody likes you. There's a reason you are all alone—no one wants to be around you. Face it—you are a creep.*

And everyone sees it! And you are fat and ugly. You are gross and unattractive. Everyone sees that, too! Gloria became sad and angry as she took in these attacks by her critical inner voice—sad because of how bad these statements made her feel, and angry because she was being addressed in such a vicious way.

Continue to verbalize your self-critical thoughts as they come to you, and always turn your "I" statements into "you" statements. They may be brutal and cruel, but it's important for you to express them.

Now look at the critical thoughts about *your partner* and *your relationship* that you became aware of in step 1. When you convert these thoughts from "I" statements to "you" statements, it will be particularly helpful for you to think of your critical inner voice as a mean coach who lives in your head and gives you advice about your partner and your relationship.

For Gloria, the thoughts "He doesn't care about me. He's at work all the time. He's not attracted to me anymore. It's like he doesn't want to be around me" became *He doesn't care about you. He's at work all the time. He's not attracted to you anymore. It's like he doesn't want to be around you.* And "I'm the one who makes the effort in this relationship. I'm the one who puts the energy into it, the one who's invested in it. If it weren't for me, Nick would be happy for it to just die out. This is just what happens after a while" became *You're the one who makes the effort in this relationship. You're the one who puts the energy into it, the one who's invested in it. If it weren't for you, Nick would be happy for it to just die out. This is just what happens after a while.*

Say these "you" statements out loud. As you do, pay attention to your feelings and thoughts. Often these attacks by your critical inner voice will activate even angrier and more intense thoughts about your partner or your relationship.

In regard to Nick, Gloria continued to change her "I" statements to "you" statements: *It's not just that he isn't interested in you—he can't stand you! He wishes you weren't here. He wants to leave you.* In regard to her relationship with Nick, her "I" statements became *Why are you pouring your energy into this relationship? Is it really worth it? You're getting nothing out of this relationship! All relationships die out, and yours is no different!*

Continue to say these "you" statements out loud. Even though they may sound mean and hurtful, verbalizing them is a valuable exercise. Why? Because this is your critical inner voice talking to you. These cruel statements express the attitudes of the enemy that operates within you. As negative thoughts come to you, and as you verbalize them in the form of "you" statements, you may have a strong reaction because you'll be feeling your critical inner voice's hostility toward you, your partner, and your relationship. Even if you feel hurt, sad, or angry about being seen and addressed from such a malicious point of view, go ahead and allow yourself to experience your emotions.

Step 3. Reflect

Step 3 of the Voice Therapy method is to *reflect* on the thoughts and insights that came up for you in step 2 when you verbalized the attacks of your critical inner voice. Step 3, which follows naturally from step 2, offers you the opportunity to think about those attacks and digest what you have just been exposed to.

In step 3, people typically realize that the critical inner voice is expressing core negative beliefs of which they've been only vaguely aware. They usually also recognize that the critical inner voice represents some way in which they were seen or treated during childhood by a particular parent, another family member, or a significant person outside the family. Sometimes the critical inner voice expresses negative views and attitudes about love and relationships that people inadvertently assimilated while growing up.

As the attacks of Gloria's critical inner voice became more hostile, that voice began to sound familiar to her. When the voice told her that she was ugly and boring, it reminded her of her mother's critical way of seeing her. Growing up, she'd felt that her mother wanted her to be prettier, smarter, and more popular. When the voice told her that Nick was rejecting her, it made her think of her father's disinterest in her. She'd felt that her father never noticed her, and she had desperately tried to get his attention and approval. Gloria began to see how the attacks of her critical inner voice were tied into her past and not reflective of her present life.

It is also common for people to have spontaneous insights into how the critical inner voice has been destructively influencing their present-day behavior. Awareness of this insidious internal process often leads to an overall feeling of clarity. As people realize the cruelty of the attitudes being directed toward them, and as they trace these attitudes to their sources in childhood, they develop compassion for themselves.

Step 4. Confront

Step 4 of the Voice Therapy method is to *confront* the attacks of the critical inner voice, responding to them with "I" statements. Once you've identified, verbalized, and reflected on the attitudes of your critical inner voice, it is necessary for you to stand up for yourself, your partner, and your relationship by confronting your internal enemy. Use "I" statements to respond directly and forcefully to the attacks of your critical inner voice and assert your own point of view.

There are two ways to do this. The first approach is more emotional and irrational; it involves freely letting go and expressing your feelings. When people first take a stand against the negative ways in which they have been viewing themselves, they often experience intense feelings, such as indignation and anger or even deep sadness. It is a good idea to be tolerant of whatever emotions arise, easily accept them, and openly express them.

Gloria answered her critical inner voice's attacks on herself: "You are always criticizing me and saying that I'm boring and unattractive! You're always telling me that nobody could love me. That's the message that you're getting across. Well, it isn't true. I'm the same person I was when Nick met me, and I'm the same person he married. I'm still interesting and fun and attractive. There's nothing wrong with me! The real truth is that all you care about is tearing me down! And that's all you've ever cared about. Shut up! I'm done listening to you!"

Gloria went on: "You have such a critical way of looking at me. You distort reality and then run me down. This has been going on for such a long time! I've been listening to you for way too long."

She answered the critical inner voice's attacks on Nick: "You are wrong about Nick, too! You distort everything to make it seem like he's going to reject me. He's been focused on work lately. He wants to get ahead because he cares about this family. He's not trying to get away from me. He misses me and the kids—he feels bad about it, and he's been talking about it. So don't grab on to it and try to make it seem like he's negligent or not interested in me. And he certainly isn't leaving me. You don't know what you're talking about!"

She defended her relationship: "Our relationship is fine! Why do you think he's working so hard? Because he cares about the quality of our life together. Don't try to make it out to be one-sided. We both care deeply about being close and maintaining our love. Our relationship isn't dying! All you care about is trying to rip us apart!"

Gloria continued: "You are always tearing him down and belittling our relationship. If I listened to your advice, I would be living all alone, with no love in my life!"

After Gloria stood up to the mistreatment she was enduring from her critical inner voice, expressed her anger, and defended Nick and their relationship, she felt some sadness opening up in her.

The second approach is more rational; when you choose this way of responding, you take an objective standpoint, call out the unreal basis of your critical inner voice's attacks, and confront it in a more logical and mature way. It's beneficial to do this after having experienced a strong emotional response to the critical inner voice's abuse. This doesn't mean that you deny your anger but only that you sort things out rationally and speak with the strength and authority of an adult.

When Gloria's sadness subsided, she calmly confronted her critical inner voice's attacks in a serious tone, starting with the voice's attacks on her: "You are not right about me. There is nothing wrong with me. My life is somewhat routine, but that doesn't mean I'm boring. And I have put on a few pounds, but that doesn't make me gross and unattractive. Nick likes me the way I am. I have no reason to feel insecure except when I'm listening to you!"

She confronted the voice's attacks on Nick: "You are so cruel! The minute there's the slightest issue, you seize on it and make it into something. Nick isn't rejecting me. He's been working hard, and I feel compassion for him. That's what love is really about—caring for someone, not attacking them, when they're going through a challenging time."

And she responded to the critical inner voice's attempt to undermine her relationship: "You always try to make me out as the victim. You always try to make this relationship look like he's a jerk and I'm a saint. It's not like that. We are two people with strengths and weaknesses who see each other realistically and care deeply for each other and about our relationship."

It can be confusing to know exactly what to say when it comes to standing up for yourself. One suggestion is to respond directly to a specific attack being launched against you. For example, Gloria told her critical inner voice that she was *not* boring or unattractive, that her body *wasn't* disgusting, and that she was *not* being rejected. In addition to saying what you *are not*, it is equally important to state what you *are*.

Gloria added, "I'm a lively person who is fun to be with. Plus, there are a lot of things that I am interested in, in addition to being a mother. And I am an attractive woman and I enjoy being sexual and affectionate."

It can also be unclear how to go about defending your partner and your relationship. Again, you can respond directly to a specific attack, as Gloria did:

Standing up for Nick, Gloria said, "He's not bored with me. He's not disinterested and wanting to leave me. He loves me and loves being with me." And standing up for her relationship, she said, "There isn't an imbalance in our relationship. I'm not the one who has to put in all the effort to make it work. Nick works hard to maintain closeness between us, too."

Again, just as it's important to say what your partner and your relationship are not, it's important to state what your partner and your relationship are.

Gloria added, "Nick's interested in me. He likes hearing what I think about and is interested in my opinions. Even when he's busy, like now, our communication is good, and we share the struggles. We both make the success and quality of our relationship a priority. I love that about him."

Step 5. Plan

Step 5 of the Voice Therapy method is to *plan* actions that will counter your critical inner voice. To pinpoint what these actions will be, it is necessary for you to review what you have learned from identifying, verbalizing, reflecting on, and confronting your critical inner voice. When you say its attacks out loud in the form of "you" statements, you expose the internal process that has been influencing your destructive behavior. Therefore, a constructive action is to disobey this voice—that is, to refuse to do what it tells you to do. In other words, you need to be aware of the directives of your critical inner voice, and then you need to make a conscious effort not to act on them.

The process of confronting your critical inner voice also sheds light on your own point of view, and on what has meaning for you; it offers insight into who you are. For example, consider what you said about yourself when you were standing up to the attacks your critical inner voice directed at you. Consider what you said when you expressed your true feelings about your partner and your relationship. Be aware of those statements, and then make a conscious effort to act on them, not on the directives of your critical inner voice.

Be very specific about which behavior you are going to stop and which behavior you are going to engage in. Formulate the details of the different actions you intend to take. If you are in therapy, you can develop a list of actions with your therapist. If you're not, you can write each action down in your journal or discuss it with a friend. Sharing your plans with your therapist or a friend, or writing them down in your journal, will help you establish concrete goals and move beyond mere wishes and dreams.

Gloria made a plan for challenging four different types of attacks that were coming from her critical inner voice and hurting her in her relationship.

She wanted to go against the voice that attacked her when she was alone. To break out of her isolation, Gloria decided to engage with more adults throughout her day. She also made it a goal to pursue her independent interests.

She wanted to ignore the voice that was telling her she was unattractive. Nick wasn't bothered by Gloria's appearance, but Gloria herself was, so she formulated a plan for losing the weight she had gained. Gloria knew that taking this action would make her feel better about herself.

She wanted to challenge the voice that said Nick was losing interest in her. She knew the truth—Nick was busy and distracted by work, which had nothing to do with her, and he still loved her—and she wanted to act on what she knew. So she decided to stop unloading her insecurities on Nick at the end of the day. Instead, she would speak with him in a personal way about herself and her goals, and she would also express her genuine interest in how his day had gone.

Finally, she wanted to counter the voice telling her that she was the only one who cared about their relationship. Gloria made a plan to stop complaining to Nick that he wasn't doing enough. Instead, she decided to focus on maximizing the time that was available to them.

Step 6. Implement

Step 6 of the Voice Therapy method is to *implement* your plans for countering your critical inner voice. Even though it seems simple and practical, this is often the most challenging step. It will take determination, discipline, and perseverance for you to stick to your plan. Fortunately, in step 5 you outlined specific types of behaviors and actions that you will adopt, and now you know exactly what to do. Regardless of anything you're thinking or feeling, your total focus now is on taking the actions you have committed yourself to carrying out.

But don't be overly ambitious. If you try to implement too many plans at once, you will be overwhelmed and have difficulty accomplishing any of them. Choose one or two goals to concentrate on. And don't have unrealistic expectations—accept that you will falter and make missteps along the way. Maintain a compassionate attitude toward yourself and what you are trying to accomplish. You are taking action to tackle long-standing, tenacious defenses that are resistant to change.

> Gloria decided to direct her first actions at improving her relationship with Nick. When he had to work on a Saturday, instead of taking his absence as a personal rejection, she reminded herself that he was as disappointed as she was. She had the idea that she and the kids could meet him for a lunchtime picnic in a park near his office. With the goal of maximizing their time together, Gloria also set aside time in the evening just for the two of them. She was sure not to be distracted or preoccupied; she wanted to take advantage of the moment and be fully present. During these times, Gloria felt relaxed and loving, and she and Nick both enjoyed the opportunity to laugh and be affectionate.
>
> Later, Gloria took action to break out of her isolation. She befriended some mothers she had met through her children's activities. And to pursue her other interests, she reached out to her former boss and offered to take on special projects that she could do from home. In the interest of feeling attractive, she made an effort to look her best. She also began to eat a healthy diet and exercise regularly.

Reactions to Challenging the Critical Inner Voice

When you challenge your critical inner voice, whether you stand up to it in words or take action against it, the voice may temporarily step up its attacks. Sometimes it predicts failure: *Who are you kidding? You're never going to change! You've tried before, and you always fail.* Or it may try to coax you into giving up: *Don't even bother trying to change! Look at how uncomfortable it's making you feel! It'd be so much easier to just go back to the way you've always been.*

In effect, the voice is being threatened, so it is fighting back. This makes sense when you consider that you are changing attitudes and behavior that have been part of your defense system for a long time. But if you can sweat it out through this period, your critical voice's intensified attacks will subside along with your feelings of anxiety and vulnerability, and you will adjust. You will gradually become comfortable as your new attitudes and behavior become a natural part of you.

Why Voice Therapy Works

Up to this point, we've been discussing how the Voice Therapy method works. But *why* does it work? In large part, Voice Therapy works because it changes the brain.

James E. Zull (2004), who wrote *The Art of Changing the Brain: Enriching the Practice of Teaching by Exploring the Biology of Learning*, citing earlier work by educational theorist David A. Kolb (1984), describes how the brain carries out four basic functions:

1. Getting information

2. Making meaning of the information

3. Creating new ideas from that meaning

4. Acting on those ideas

These four basic brain functions can be mapped to the three learning components of Voice Therapy, as shown in the following table:

Basic Brain Functions	Learning Components of Voice Therapy
1. Get information	1. Identify and catalog self-critical thoughts and attacks by the critical inner voice
2. Make meaning of information 3. Create new ideas from meaning	2. Form insights into self-critical thoughts and respond to them
4. Act on ideas	3. Make plans and take action against self-critical thoughts

In order to change, people have to rewire their brains. At the beginning of the chapter, we looked at some recent discoveries in neuroscience. Other key findings by neuroscientists point to two key elements that are necessary before change can be brought about in the brain's networks of neurons (Zull 2004): *practice* and *emotion*.

Practice

Every action either strengthens or weakens connections in the brain. The more often neurons are used, the more frequently they fire, and the stronger their connections become. Neurons that are rarely or never used eventually die. Therefore, any action strengthens the existing pathways in the brain, and if the actions are new actions, they build new pathways. In other words, neurons change in response to practice—that is, new actions performed over and over—a process that requires persistence.

Voice Therapy enables you to identify the actions that will successfully rewire your brain. For one thing, when you can pinpoint destructive behavior that is instigated by your critical inner voice, you gain clarity about which behavior you need to stop in order to weaken those old connections in the brain between your critical inner voice and the destructive behavior. In addition, identifying behavior that reflects your real point of view is a way to highlight the actions you should practice in order to strengthen positive connections between your thoughts and your behavior and lay down new neural pathways that will lead to permanent change.

Emotion

The experience of emotion has a double impact: it causes neurons to fire, and it causes the release of adrenaline, serotonin, and dopamine in the brain. These emotional chemicals stimulate change in the brain's circuitry, helping neuronal networks become stronger, larger, and more complex (Schore 2003b; Welling 2012).

In Voice Therapy, as a fundamental part of the therapeutic process, the emphasis is on becoming aware of emotions and then expressing them. In step 2, for example, when you verbalize your self-critical thoughts and the attacks of your critical inner voice, powerful feelings are aroused in you, and this happens again in step 4, when you confront your critical inner voice. The process of experiencing and releasing strong emotions leaves you more vulnerable and emotionally open, more deeply understanding of yourself, and more integrated as a person.

Journaling and the Voice Therapy Method

As we've just seen, emotion combined with constructive action provides the necessary stimulus for personal growth. The best way to rewire your brain and change your negative thought processes is to work with a counselor or a psychotherapist. But you can also make progress on your own, and journaling is a useful tool if you want to go solo.

Remember to take your time—this is not something to be powered through. You'll probably be feeling many emotions and having a lot of insights as you work through the six steps of Voice Therapy. Be sensitive to yourself, take a break if you need one, give yourself a chance to process what you are experiencing and learning, and seek professional help if you run into painful problems while working alone. Spend the time you need on each step to do it justice. If you hurry, you won't get everything you can out of the process.

The following journal exercises lead you through the first five steps of Voice Therapy, which have been adapted for journaling: identifying (and writing out) thoughts that are critical of you, your partner, and your relationship; rewriting those thoughts (rather than saying them out loud); reflecting on them; confronting them; and planning actions to counter them. For each of these exercises, you may want to start out using the attacks by the critical inner voice that you uncovered in the chapter 2 journal exercises. Write freely. Let your thoughts flow out of you and onto the paper (or screen), and pay no attention to form, style, or principles of composition. The purpose of writing in your journal is to record your thoughts and responses as they come to you.

Journal Exercise 3.1. Your Critical Inner Voice Versus You in Your Relationship

1. *Identify* your critical thoughts about yourself in your relationship, using "I" statements. Write these statements down in your journal.

2. *Rewrite* your "I" statements as "you" statements in the form of attacks coming from your critical inner voice. Expand on them, continuing to rewrite them as "you" statements.

3. *Reflect* on what you have written, and record any new thoughts and insights.

4. *Confront* the attacks coming from your critical inner voice, using "I" statements to stand up for yourself.

5. *Plan* the actions you will take to counter your critical inner voice, and write these actions down, being detailed and specific about what you will do with respect to particular people, communication, behavior, situations, and so on. (You will *implement* your plan in step 6 of Voice Therapy.)

Journal Exercise 3.2. Your Critical Inner Voice Versus Your Partner in Your Relationship

1. *Identify* your critical thoughts about your partner in your relationship, using "I" statements. Write these statements down in your journal.

2. *Rewrite* your "I" statements as "you" statements in the form of attacks coming from your critical inner voice. Expand on them, continuing to rewrite them as "you" statements.

3. *Reflect* on what you have written, and record any new thoughts and insights.

4. *Confront* the attacks coming from your critical inner voice, using "I" statements to stand up for yourself.

5. *Plan* the actions you will take to counter your critical inner voice, and write these actions down, being detailed and specific about what you will do with respect to particular people, communication, behavior, situations, and so on. (You will *implement* your plan in step 6 of Voice Therapy.)

Journal Exercise 3.3. Your Critical Inner Voice Versus Your Relationship

1. *Identify* your critical thoughts about your relationship, using "I" statements. Write these statements down in your journal.

2. *Rewrite* your "I" statements as "you" statements in the form of attacks coming from your critical inner voice. Expand on them, continuing to rewrite them as "you" statements.

3. *Reflect* on what you have written, and record any new thoughts and insights.

4. *Confront* the attacks coming from your critical inner voice, using "I" statements to stand up for yourself.

5. *Plan* the actions you will take to counter your critical inner voice, and write these actions down, being detailed and specific about what you will do with respect to particular people, communication, behavior, situations, and so on. (You will *implement* your plan in step 6 of Voice Therapy.)

Summary and a Look Ahead

"Stay out of your head," a popular saying goes—it's a "bad neighborhood to hang out in alone" (Ciotti n.d.). Voice Therapy helps you stay out of your head. It keeps you from being distracted by your critical inner voice and its destructive attitude toward you and your life. In effect, Voice Therapy operates as a neighborhood watch for your mind by identifying and challenging the internal enemy that makes your head an unsafe place to be.

The critical inner voice can never be completely eliminated. It can be quieted for a time, but there are periods when it is more active. It can be dormant or in remission, but it can never be totally eradicated. Nevertheless, Voice Therapy gives you a method for challenging your critical inner voice when it' attacks you, your partner, or your relationship. You can use the tools presented in this chapter to become aware of how your internal enemy drives your negative attitudes and behavior. Then, with this awareness, you can counter the dictates of your critical inner voice and take the necessary actions to preserve your intimate relationship. And when the inevitable missteps and setbacks occur, you can use Voice Therapy to help you foster a compassionate attitude toward yourself. That will support you in staying strong and not giving up.

Take inspiration from Abraham Maslow (1968, 47), a founder of humanistic psychology, who described healthy growth as "a never ending series of free choice situations, confronting each individual at every point throughout his life, in which he must choose between the delights of safety and growth, dependence and independence, regression and progression, immaturity and maturity." You *can* make the daring choices you need to make in order to overcome your internal obstacles to love. One such obstacle, a major one for most people, is fear of being vulnerable—the topic of the next chapter.

CHAPTER 4

When Love Makes Us Feel Vulnerable

Love is not love until love's vulnerable.

> —Theodore Roethke, "The Dream,"
> in *Words for the Wind: Poems of*
> *Theodore Roethke*

Everything about love induces us to be vulnerable. Suddenly we find ourselves being softer and more open. We are surprised by our feelings of tenderness and compassion for others. We are unexplainably optimistic about life. Part of what feels so good about love is that it feels so good to feel trusting and safe enough to let our guard down.

Nevertheless, this exposure can also feel scary. It is frightening to find yourself without the protection of your customary defenses. This chapter explains how we tend to vacillate between embracing being vulnerable and being frightened by it and then defending against it. As we open ourselves to being loving and loved, our vulnerability makes us increasingly anxious. And once we have found love, there is a fear of losing it. In these situations, without knowing why, we may engage in behavior that pushes love away to relieve our fear and anxiety. This chapter looks at behavior we often use to keep from being vulnerable, and at behavior we can engage in to be more vulnerable. Some of the chapter's journal exercises will help you recognize behavior that keeps you defended as well as the critical inner voice that supports it. Other journal exercises will assist you in planning actions that will encourage you to remain vulnerable to love.

Defenses Against Vulnerability

Most people consider being vulnerable an unsafe state to be in. But there are also positive aspects of vulnerability. In her book *Daring Greatly*, the sociologist Brené Brown writes, "Vulnerability is the core of all emotions and feelings. To feel is to be vulnerable. To believe vulnerability is weakness is to believe that feelings are weakness" (Brown 2012, 33). Being vulnerable to feeling and to the possibility of being hurt is actually an adaptive position to take because it increases the probability of finding and maintaining love as well as of achieving overall gratification and satisfaction in life. However, remaining vulnerable isn't easy.

People often have specific defensive reactions to feeling vulnerable in a relationship. They may try to establish a more comfortable distance by withdrawing emotionally or physically from their partner and isolating themselves. They might attempt to minimize the love that is being directed toward them by controlling their partner's loving responses with obvious (or not so obvious) negative reactions and manipulations. They can withhold the qualities their partner especially appreciates or they can minimize their own loving responses by denying themselves the pleasure and fulfillment they once experienced in being close.

Isolation

People often defend against feeling vulnerable by seeking isolation. At these times, they withdraw into themselves and limit interpersonal contact; they become remote and inaccessible. Their focus is inward, toward themselves, instead of outward, toward their loved one. They no longer engage in the exchanges between two people that are an intrinsic feature of intimacy, and their ability to give and accept love is seriously impaired. This is illustrated in the example of Henry;

the depth of his love for his wife and their newborn son increased his feelings of vulnerability, and he began to isolate himself from his family:

> As a child, Henry primarily kept to himself. As a teenager, he rarely dated, and as a young adult, he was isolated and depressed. Then he joined the army, and for the first time he was sociable and enjoyed the company of friends. Afterward he moved to California, where he made some friends at work and was generally happy.
>
> Soon he met Catherine. They were eventually married, and a few years later their son, Billy, was born. Henry was surprised by his joy in being a father and his delight in having a family of his own.
>
> During the year after Billy's birth, Henry began to struggle once again with his tendency toward isolation. Rather than spend his free time with Catherine and Billy, he chose to work alone in his shop or hike by himself in the nearby mountains. Following a particularly solitary weekend, Catherine told him that she was worried about his increasing isolation, and his response was angry: "I like being by myself. I like building things. I like going off by myself. Don't mess with me. This is who I am."
>
> Catherine mentioned to Henry that he seemed depressed and irritable the more he was alone. She felt that he was pulling away from her and Billy, and she expressed her feelings of missing him.

Journal Exercise 4.1. How You Isolate Yourself

Consider the following questions. When your answer is yes, write the question and your answer in your journal. Elaborate with any other thoughts and ideas you may have on the topic. Your answers will indicate some of the ways you may be isolating yourself in your relationship.

- Have I been isolating myself lately?
- Do I have a tendency to isolate myself?
- Did I spend a lot of time alone as a child?
- In what ways did I specifically isolate myself as a child?
- What are the specific ways I isolate myself today?
- When I am alone, how do I spend my time?
- Do I have any inward habits?
- Do I tend to choose isolated activities over being social?
- Does my partner complain that I am distant and unavailable?

Just as the critical inner voice supports all of our defenses, it encourages isolation. Because the retreat from intimacy is unconscious, it is hard to see that the critical inner voice is behind it. People never say to themselves, "Well, I'm uncomfortable being so in love—it's time to be less close now." Yet they might find themselves thinking things like "I need my own space" or "I need some time alone to chill" or simply "I'm too busy" or "I'm too stressed" or "I'm too tired." These types of thoughts can be translated into attacks by the critical inner voice: *You're so busy (stressed, tired, …) that you need to take some time by yourself. You need a break from people and your relationship.* Looking into this sort of inimical coaching will help you gain access to the critical inner voice that is instigating your isolation. You can also be aware of the inner voice that is critical of your partner: *Why can't she just leave you alone? She's so demanding and dependent! Do you have to spend all of your time together?*

Henry used the steps of Voice Therapy to understand his defensive reaction of isolating himself:

When Henry calmed down, he was able to apply Voice Therapy, turn his defensive responses to Catherine into "you" statements, and recognize them as coming from his inner critical voice: *You like being by yourself. You like building things. You like going off by yourself. Don't let her tell you otherwise! This is who you are.* He expanded on these "you" statements in relation to Catherine: *What's her problem? She's such a nag! She doesn't even know you. For you, making something or going off in nature is much more gratifying than just hanging around with someone. You're good alone! This is who you are.*

When Henry thought about these statements from his critical inner voice, he recognized that this voice had been with him ever since he was a child. This realization helped Henry conceptualize how he wanted to answer the voice's attacks: "I'm not a loner. I didn't like being alone as a kid—it was just the situation I found myself in. I like having friends. I love being with my family. I'm a social person. You have me all wrong! And you have Catherine wrong, too. She's not needy or possessive. She just likes being with me, and she cares about how I feel."

Journal Exercise 4.2. How Your Critical Inner Voice Promotes Isolation

Using your responses to journal exercise 4.1, choose one of your primary ways of isolating yourself. Then follow the first four adapted steps of the Voice Therapy method.

1. *Identify* your thoughts about yourself in relation to isolation, using "I" statements. For example, what thoughts about yourself or your partner justify and support this defensive behavior? Write these statements down in your journal.

2. *Rewrite* your "I" statements as "you" statements in the form of attacks coming from your critical inner voice. Expand on them, continuing to rewrite them as "you" statements.

3. *Reflect* on what you have written, and record any new thoughts and insights.

4. *Confront* the attacks coming from your critical inner voice, using "I" statements to stand up for yourself.

Isolation is a dangerous defensive reaction. It is different from time spent in relaxing self-contemplation, constructive planning, or creative endeavors. This type of alone time is the perfect breeding ground for self-destructive attitudes and behavior. It is characterized by an increase in critical negative thoughts toward yourself and your partner as well as by self-destructive behavior and habits. In isolation, you can become careless about your emotional well-being. When isolation is extreme, it has been shown to be not just a significant indicator of suicidal intent but also a central element of completed suicidal acts.

Controlling Behavior

Some people react against being vulnerable by attempting to control the partner and the relationship in order to maintain distance. This type of control is usually manifested in one of two ways: through obvious, overt actions or through subtle, covert manipulations. Both maneuvers can arouse fear and/or guilt in a partner.

When people exert overt control, they typically influence the loved one through parental behavior that is authoritarian and condescending and that indicates approval and disapproval. Some people try to intimidate the partner with verbal threats of rejection or abandonment. Others impose emotional or even physical punishment.

When people exert covert control, they attempt to regulate the loved one's responses through guilt-provoking behavior that is indirect yet wields considerable power over the other. This tyranny of weakness is highly effective. For example, a partner who identifies as a victim or is self-denying can easily maneuver the other partner. Irrational or self-destructive behavior is also intimidating. This is a type of emotional terrorism that makes one partner accountable for the unhappiness of the other. Where this type of behavior is concerned, threats of self-harm or actual suicide clearly have the most impact.

Whether attempts to control a partner's emotions and behavior are overt or covert, they inflict long-term harm on the dignity and self-respect of the partner who is being controlled as well as on the partner who is doing the controlling. Emotional blackmail can be effective, but it is not worth the price that ultimately has to be paid by the blackmailer.

Journal Exercise 4.3. How You Are Controlling in Your Relationship

Consider the following questions. When your answer is yes, write the question and your answer in your journal. Elaborate with any other thoughts and ideas you may have on the topic. Your answers will indicate some of the ways you may be controlling in your relationship.

- Are there any obvious ways in which I am controlling?

- Are there times when I behave in a dominating or parental way with my partner?

- Can I be bossy?

- Do I have a tendency to take charge of everything?

- Can I be punishing when things don't go my way?

- Are there any subtle ways in which I am controlling?

- Are there times when I withdraw affection or act cold if I don't get my way?

- Do I sometimes sulk and pout if I don't get what I want?

- Do I ever play the victim in relation to my partner?

- Do I tend to act helpless and weak?

The critical inner voice supports both types of controlling behavior with warnings not to be vulnerable. When its message is about you and your partner, it encourages you to be guarded and distrustful. It cautions you that when you are vulnerable, you are operating from a weak position: *You are exposing yourself to being hurt. You have to protect* yourself and maintain control of the situation at all times. It predicts that your partner will control you: *If you are vulnerable, he will have the upper hand and exploit you. If you put yourself in a weak position, he won't respect you.* It forecasts that you will be humiliated and made a fool of: *People are going to think you are a wimp. How will you be able to face people when she rejects you?* This kind of critical inner voice influences you to take direct or indirect action in order to exert control in your relationship.

Journal Exercise 4.4. How Your Critical Inner Voice Supports Controlling Behavior

Using your responses to journal exercise 4.3, select one of your primary ways of acting controlling in your relationship. Then follow the first four adapted steps of the Voice Therapy method.

1. *Identify* your thoughts about yourself in relation to your controlling behavior, using "I" statements. For example, what thoughts about yourself or your partner justify and support this defensive behavior? Write these statements down in your journal.

2. *Rewrite* your "I" statements as "you" statements in the form of attacks coming from your critical inner voice. Expand on them, continuing to rewrite them as "you" statements.

3. *Reflect* on what you have written, and record any new thoughts and insights.

4. *Confront* the attacks coming from your critical inner voice, using "I" statements to stand up for yourself.

Withholding

People often protect themselves from being vulnerable and regulate the degree of love and closeness in an intimate relationship by withholding the very behavior and traits the partner especially values.

If a couple enjoys joking around together, one partner just has to stop being cheerful and easygoing, and suddenly the two of them won't be having as much fun. If a couple is typically affectionate, one partner need only become reserved and a little cooler, and the affection between them will quickly chill. If a couple enjoys sharing activities, one partner can become somewhat less engaged and less available, and soon they will find themselves spending less time together. Withholding has an insidious effect on a relationship: it progressively deadens the feelings of excitement, passion, and attraction that both partners originally felt for one another.

In everyday situations, it is easy to recognize a wide variety of withholding behavior that men and women engage in; in fact, such behavior is so common that many people accept it as normal. For some people, withholding can mean being habitually late, procrastinating in the performance of a promised task, disregarding the family budget, or failing to share the responsibilities of childrearing. For others, withholding can mean putting on too much weight or failing to keep enough weight on. Withholding can also take the form of simply not smiling or being congenial.

Whatever its form, withholding is largely unconscious and is manifested primarily in passive behavior, and this is why withholding is so complicated to confront directly. Withholding creates distance between partners and undermines their feelings for one another as love and caring come to be replaced by resentment and hostility. In addition, having something withheld from you by your loved one can provoke intense longing and desperation in you for what is being denied. It can even cause you to turn against yourself.

Journal Exercise 4.5. How You Withhold in Your Relationship

Consider the following questions. When your answer is yes, write the question and your answer in your journal. Elaborate with any other thoughts and ideas you may have on the topic. Your answers will indicate some of the ways you may be withholding in your relationship.

- Do I no longer behave in ways that my partner particularly liked?

- Did I use to be more fun, more attractive, more verbally engaged, more active, more affectionate, or more independent?

- Are there activities that we used to share that I no longer participate in?

The critical inner voice fosters withholding by promoting the view that you are being taken advantage of and victimized by your partner: *Why are you doing that for him? Why can't he do it for himself? Does he expect these kinds of services from you?* The critical inner voice also coaches you to be self-protective rather than loving and generous, and to hold back on the expression of your positive feelings: *What about your needs? You have to pay attention to yourself!* And this voice makes you self-conscious with warnings like *Other people don't act like this. You look like a pathetic fool! You're degrading yourself. Have some dignity!*

Journal Exercise 4.6. How Your Critical Inner Voice Encourages Withholding

Using your responses to journal exercise 4.5, select one of your primary ways of withholding in your relationship. Then follow the first four adapted steps of the Voice Therapy method.

1. *Identify* your thoughts about yourself in relation to your withholding behavior, using "I" statements. For example, what thoughts about yourself or your partner justify and support this defensive behavior? Write these statements down in your journal.

2. *Rewrite* your "I" statements as "you" statements in the form of attacks coming from your critical inner voice. Expand on them, continuing to rewrite them as "you" statements.

3. *Reflect* on what you have written, and record any new thoughts and insights.

4. *Confront* the attacks coming from your critical inner voice, using "I" statements to stand up for yourself.

Sexual Withholding

Because withholding is a defensive reaction against love and intimacy, it is understandable that it can be a significant factor in sexual relating, too, and can lead to the development of sexual problems between partners. Sexual withholding takes the form of holding back or inhibiting sexual desire and its expressions, such as touching and physical affection, maintaining physical attractiveness, and other aspects of natural sexuality. When one partner becomes less responsive, the other often reacts by feeling emotionally hungry, insecure, or angry. This can create a pattern of desperation and resistance between the partners. Although this type of withholding takes place "in the bedroom," its damaging effects are not contained there. They are widespread and permeate other sectors of the couple's life.

Journal Exercise 4.7. How You Are Sexually Withholding in Your Relationship

Consider the following questions. When your answer is yes, write the question and your answer in your journal. Elaborate with any other thoughts and ideas you may have on the topic. Your answers will indicate some of the ways you may be sexually withholding in your intimate relationship.

- Do I ever feel sexually inhibited or constrained?

- Are there ways in which I've changed from how I used to be in my sexual relationship?

- Am I less active or affectionate or passionate?

- Do we make love less frequently?

- Have I let myself go physically or neglected my appearance?

- Do I tend to avoid being sexual?

The critical inner voice that supports sexual withholding is similar to the one that supports all other types of withholding behavior. It promotes the view that you are being victimized: *Why does he always want to have sex? It's all about sex with him.* Or it expresses a protective, coddling attitude: *You're too tired. Is this what you really want? It's so much effort!* It also promotes such conventional rationalizations as *It's natural to feel less sexual as a relationship matures* or *All men care about is sex* or *Women don't really want sex.*

Journal Exercise 4.8. How Your Critical Inner Voice Encourages Sexual Withholding

Using your responses to journal exercise 4.7, select one of your primary ways of withholding in your sexual relationship. Then follow the first four adapted steps of the Voice Therapy method.

1. *Identify* your thoughts about yourself in relation to your sexually withholding behavior, using "I" statements. For example, what thoughts about yourself or your partner justify and support this defensive behavior? Write these statements down in your journal.

2. *Rewrite* your "I" statements as "you" statements in the form of attacks coming from your critical inner voice. Expand on them, continuing to rewrite them as "you" statements.

3. *Reflect* on what you have written, and record any new thoughts and insights.

4. *Confront* the attacks coming from your critical inner voice, using "I" statements to stand up for yourself.

For the most part, we do not intentionally withhold our affection or our sexual responses in a calculated, deliberately hurtful manipulation. We are largely unaware that our sexual withholding is causing pain and distress to ourselves and our partner. However, much of the suffering and conflict between partners is due to the fact that the love, affection, and sexual responses they once felt and expressed are being held back by one or both of them.

How to Be Vulnerable to Love

Vulnerability is a trendy topic these days. At the time of this writing, a video of Brené Brown's TED talk "The Power of Vulnerability" (Brown 2010) had more than 30 million views. Even greeting cards and posters now tout the benefits of being vulnerable. In fact, the term "vulnerability" risks losing its meaning and becoming a cliché through overuse. Nevertheless, the sheer intensity of popular interest in vulnerability shows that it's a subject that resonates with many people. Vulnerability is a worthy goal, but being vulnerable can be challenging.

You can become and remain vulnerable in your intimate relationship by recognizing and challenging your defensive behavior as well as the critical inner voice that supports it; both leave you guarded and suspicious of love. To achieve this, you can plan actions to counteract the ways in which you push love away, and you can implement constructive behavior that supports your being vulnerable.

When you first initiate this constructive behavior, you will probably experience an increase in the attacks coming from your critical inner voice. In effect, you are taking that voice on when you disobey it and act against its directives, and it will probably retaliate with a renewed barrage of attacks in an effort to regain the upper hand. It may call you a fool. It may advise you to be careful and protect yourself. It may warn you that you are putting yourself in a position to be hurt or taken advantage of. But if you are steadfast in your resolve to disregard its attacks, and if you maintain your plan of action, then your critical inner voice will eventually subside, and change will occur. If you persevere, you will win the battle.

Stop Behavior That Keeps You from Being Vulnerable

One benefit of uncovering how your critical inner voice is directing your life is that you can see the negative actions you need to stop in order to overcome it. You can use this information to challenge your defensive acts of isolating, controlling, and withholding. Once Henry identified how his critical inner voice was encouraging his isolation, he saw clearly what he had to do in order to counteract his tendency to be alone:

Henry decided to spend his weekends being more social. The following Saturday night, he and Catherine had friends over for dinner. They also made a plan to set aside an afternoon every weekend to spend with their son, and they had fun with him at the zoo that Sunday afternoon. Henry also decided to involve others in his previously solo activities and interests. He sent an email to friends and family members, encouraging them to join him on an upcoming hike. Henry became much happier in his life. He was also touched by his wife's concern and support.

Journal Exercise 4.9. Planning for Action Against the Critical Inner Voice That Promotes Isolation, Controlling Behavior, and Withholding

Using your responses to the previous journal exercises, think about the defensive behavior you uncovered, and about the critical inner voice that supports this behavior. Also think about what you said when you stood up for yourself and confronted your critical inner voice. Then, with these thoughts in mind, follow step 5 of Voice Therapy and *plan* the actions you will take to counter the critical inner voice that promotes isolation, controlling behavior, and withholding. Write these actions down, being detailed and specific about what you will do with respect to particular people, communication, behavior, situations, and so on. You will *implement* your plan in step 6 of Voice Therapy.

Take Action to Be Vulnerable

Not only is it important to stop behavior that interferes with being vulnerable, but it's also important to initiate behavior that fosters vulnerability. There are three things you can do that are particularly effective in developing vulnerability: you can be generous, you can ask for what you want, and you can express and accept affection. These actions don't just foster vulnerability; they also counteract the defenses that work to destroy vulnerability. Being generous discourages your withholding behavior, asking for what you want interferes with your isolating behavior, and expressing and accepting affection inhibits your controlling behavior.

BE GENEROUS

Being generous—that is, giving freely of yourself, your time, and your energy—kindles vulnerability. Generosity is an outward expression of sensitivity and compassion toward your partner. The empathy and understanding that are fundamental to being truly generous also sustain the vulnerability of both the giver and the receiver. When an act of generosity grows out of this type of attunement to and appreciation of your partner's uniqueness, it gratifies both of you.

Generosity is also effective in counteracting your withholding behavior. When you extend consideration and kindness in response to your partner's needs, as an expression of compassion and empathy, you interrupt the withholding pattern that restricts emotional exchanges between you. Therefore, it is advisable to make an effort to be giving in situations where you would normally withhold. It is also important to be generous without any expectation of reciprocal treatment. If your actions are designed to create an obligation, garner favor, or maintain a superior position, then they are not truly generous and will ultimately be hurtful to you and your partner.

Acts of generosity can take many forms. Money and other material gifts are the most easily measurable forms, but they can have less emotional and psychological impact than other types of generosity. Generous people actively look for opportunities to respond to a need in friends and loved ones. Generosity is expressed by the willingness to drop anything to do a favor or lend a hand. It can be as simple as listening when someone needs to talk.

In a close relationship, acts of generosity involve an equal exchange between partners, with benevolence on one side and receptiveness on the other. By this definition, receiving is also a generous action—it is an act of love to graciously accept and appreciate affection, kind deeds, or assistance.

Being generous with your words, your time, and your affection is not just an antidote to withholding behavior. It can also help you overcome a negative self-image as well as a cynical, distrustful attitude toward others. Altruistic actions increase feelings of self-esteem and make us feel worthwhile.

Giving to others tends to leave us feeling liberated, energized, and less defended. We also feel more satisfied in our relationships. Aside from being a moral way to live, being generous and giving is essential to our emotional well-being. Take the example of Lisa, who decided to be more generous in her relationship:

Lisa had become withholding in her relationship with Mitch. Originally, the two of them had enjoyed many common interests and shared activities. In fact, Lisa had referred to Mitch as a kindred spirit. But over time, and especially after they were married, Lisa changed. She became less inclined to talk and express her opinions, and Mitch missed their lively conversations. She also became less adventurous, wanting to stay home instead of joining Mitch in the activities they had enjoyed before. Even when Mitch suggested doing something related to one of Lisa's personal interests, she turned him down. She became aware that she was withdrawing from him and was withholding in their relationship.

This awareness helped her identify her critical inner voice, which was encouraging her defensive behavior. It attacked Mitch: *Why doesn't he leave you alone? And why do you have to do everything with him? He's so demanding!* And it attacked Lisa herself: *What about you? What about your interests? What are you, some kind of faithful puppy dog?* But Lisa confronted her critical inner voice. She stood up for herself, Mitch, and their relationship: "Mitch isn't forcing his interests on me—he's never done that. These are things I enjoy, things we're both interested in. And I'm happiest when we're sharing these activities and spending time together."

Lisa thought that being generous with Mitch would be a good way to take action against the critical inner voice that was holding her back. She decided to be generous with her words, so she made a point of expressing her thoughts and opinions. She decided to be generous with her actions, so she rejoined Mitch in the activities they had once participated in together. She decided to be generous with her affection, so she became more flirtatious and loving toward him in their intimate relationship.

At first these actions took effort, and at times Lisa felt anxious and awkward, but over time it became easier for her to initiate behavior that represented who she was and indicated her feelings for Mitch. As for Mitch, he was delighted that Lisa was "back," as he said. And Lisa was happy and relieved to feel more herself than she had in a long time.

Journal Exercise 4.10. How You Can Be More Generous

Consider the following questions. Write down any thoughts or ideas that these questions bring up for you. Doing this can help you formulate a plan for being more generous in your relationship.

- Do I have a generous attitude toward my partner?

- What opportunities do I have to be helpful to my partner?

- Can I be more available to do a favor or lend a hand?

- Do I often ask my partner how I can be of help?

- Am I empathetic toward my partner, for the most part?

- Am I basically aware of my partner's unique feelings and interests?

- Are there ways I respond to my partner's individual interests?

- How might I be more responsive to my partner's interests?

Journal Exercise 4.11. Planning for Action to Become More Generous Toward Your Partner

Using your responses to journal exercise 4.10, think about becoming more generous toward your partner. Then, with these thoughts in mind, follow step 5 of Voice Therapy and *plan* the actions you will take to become more generous. Write these actions down, being detailed and specific about what you will do with respect to particular people, communication, behavior, situations, and so on. You will *implement* your plan in step 6 of Voice Therapy.

ASK FOR WHAT YOU WANT

Asking for what you want helps you be vulnerable. It challenges your self-protective defense of being isolated because it forces you to turn to someone else to gratify your needs. It disrupts the self-indulgent habits that thrive in isolation and the critical inner voice that supports these habits when it says, for example, *You can take care of yourself— you don't need anything from anyone else.*

Asking for what you want is difficult for many people because feelings of shame often accompany wanting or needing something from another person. Shame is a painful, primitive emotion that originates in early childhood from incidents when basic needs were not fulfilled. These incidents leave children feeling deeply ashamed of their desire for affection and for wanting to be touched, loved, seen, and understood. To avoid the humiliation of ever again feeling unloved or being seen as unlovable, children become desperate to cover up any signs of wanting, and as adults they continue to expect humiliation and shaming if they ask for what they want.

In your relationship, you cannot be vulnerable unless you are willing to overcome your resistance to asking directly for what you want. Making a direct request for what you want allows your partner to know you and know what to offer you. Being vulnerable involves being willing to risk rejection, disappointment, or frustration. And there's a valuable lesson to be learned from asking directly for what you want: it's that, as an adult, you can tolerate being disappointed or frustrated when a request is declined. Asking directly for what you want will make you stronger as you become increasingly aware that you are no longer that helpless child who once suffered shame and humiliation.

Another benefit of being aware of what you want is that when you know what you want and have a feeling for what you need, you know who you are. Without awareness of your basic wants and needs, you have no way of knowing what is important or meaningful to you, and therefore no way of guiding your life. Knowing what you want is fundamental to realizing yourself as an individual, and asking for what you want is crucial to maintaining your vulnerability in your relationship.

Journal Exercise 4.12. How You Can Ask for What You Want

Consider the following questions. Write down any thoughts or ideas that these questions bring up for you. Doing this can help you formulate a plan for asking for what you want.

- What do I want, not necessarily in material terms but in terms of what I find meaningful and emotionally gratifying?

- Am I comfortable asking for what I want?

- Do I often feel shy or awkward? Am I silent or indirect?

- What do I feel too uncomfortable or too shy to ask for?

- What is my most secret want?

- Do I usually feel comfortable asking for what I want sexually?

- When being sexual, what have I wanted that I haven't told my partner about?

Journal Exercise 4.13. Planning for Action to Ask for What You Want

Using your responses to journal exercise 4.12, think about your wants and desires. Then, with these thoughts in mind, follow step 5 of Voice Therapy and *plan* the actions you will take to ask for what you want. Write these actions down, being detailed and specific about what you will do with respect to particular people, communication, behavior, situations, and so on. You will *implement* your plan in step 6 of Voice Therapy.

EXPRESS AND ACCEPT AFFECTION

When you offer and accept affection in your intimate relationship, you encourage your vulnerability and discourage your controlling defenses. As both you and your partner participate in the mutual give-and-take of loving exchanges, neither of you is likely to exert control over the other. When you are freely giving, and when you are receptive to affection that is tender, caring, playful, and seductive, you are open and undefended with your partner. Affection, both verbal and physical, is an outward expression of generosity and a reflection of asking for needs and desires to be fulfilled.

The act of making love is the most direct, intimate physical and emotional exchange possible between two people. Being fully engaged in this experience involves giving and receiving physical affection and enjoying the deeply emotional transaction that occurs during a sexual experience. Sexuality is a positive offering of pleasure to your partner and for yourself and is vital to your sense of fulfillment in your intimate relationship.

Journal Exercise 4.14. How You Can Express and Accept More Affection

Consider the following questions. Write down any thoughts or ideas that these questions bring up for you. Doing this can help you formulate a plan for expressing and accepting more affection.

- Is it easy for me to be affectionate?

- Do I express affection toward my partner?

- Could I be more affectionate?

- Are there times when I feel free to express affection and other times when I feel more self-conscious and hold back?

- Am I comfortable with my partner being affectionate toward me?

- Do I ever discourage my partner from expressing affection for me?

- Could I be more accepting and encouraging of my partner's expressions of affection?

- Are there times when I feel more comfortable with my partner's expressions of affection and times when I do not?

Journal Exercise 4.15. Planning for Action to Express and Accept More Affection

Using your responses to journal exercise 4.14, think about giving and receiving affection in your relationship. Then, with these thoughts in mind, follow step 5 of Voice Therapy and *plan* the actions you will take to be more giving and more accepting of affection. Write these actions down, being detailed and specific about what you will do with respect to particular people, communication, behavior, situations, and so on. You will *implement* your plan in step 6 of Voice Therapy.

Summary and a Look Ahead

Remaining open and nondefensive in our intimate relationship can scare us and make us feel anxious and self-protective. It's a challenge, but we can rise to it by confronting our defensive behavior and the critical inner voice that supports it. We can become and remain vulnerable by resisting our destructive behavior (such as isolating ourselves, attempting to control our partner, or withholding ourselves from our partner) and developing constructive behavior (such as being generous, asking for what we want, and expressing and accepting affection). No matter how difficult it may be to become and remain vulnerable, the goal is ultimately worth the effort. Only when we break through our defenses and remain vulnerable can we restore loving, mutually pleasurable, rewarding interactions with our partner. And only that kind of love can counter the seductions and dangers of the fantasy bond, as we'll see in the next chapter.

CHAPTER 5

When Love Disrupts the Fantasy Bond

The fantasy bond is ... a mirage. There are oases. They are to be found, sometimes, by some of us. But we shall never find an oasis in the spell of the mirage.

—R. D. Laing, foreword to Robert
W. Firestone, *The Fantasy Bond:
Structure of Psychological Defenses*

The illusion of being merged with another person is what Robert calls the *fantasy bond* (R. Firestone 1984, 1985). This illusion is originally formed in early childhood with a parent or caregiver. It serves as a defense by helping the young child maintain a feeling of safety and security when he or she is scared, hurt, or frustrated. In adulthood, when the reality of loving and being loved makes us feel vulnerable and causes us anxiety, we often try to protect ourselves by pushing love away and reestablishing this old defense—we bring the fantasy bond into our relationship and replace real love with a fantasy of love. This chapter examines how the fantasy bond is developed in childhood and then continues to operate in adult life. The chapter also discusses the fantasy bond's past and current identifiable manifestations. The fantasy bond is often difficult to detect, but certain types of behavior indicate that it is operating in a relationship. The journal exercises in this chapter will help you identify how you engage in these types of behavior, recognize the critical inner voice that encourages the behavior, and take action to challenge it.

How the Fantasy Bond Develops and Continues

As we saw in chapter 1, children develop methods of coping emotionally when they inevitably experience frustration, fear, or pain. Some of the most traumatic experiences occur in infancy, when a helpless baby is completely dependent on a parent for getting its basic needs met. Because the infant lacks any sense of time and knows only the intensity of the moment, it can suffer extreme separation anxiety. In an attempt to alleviate this emotional pain and restore a bond with the mother, the infant develops a fantasy of being merged with her, believing itself to magically be one with its mother. The primary purpose of the fantasy bond, as noted earlier, is to provide the illusion of having needs met. This defense usually involves self-soothing, calming behavior that offers some relief, such as sucking a thumb or fingers, rubbing a blanket, stroking a stuffed animal, or twirling a lock of hair. But as children grow older and less dependent on their parents, the fantasy bond persists, and the necessary self-calming adaptations of infancy often evolve into sophisticated ways for a child to numb feelings and cut off emotional pain.

Children eventually grow into adults, but remnants of the original fantasy bond persist. Its manifestations involve self-indulgent, self-pitying, self-destructive behavior, attitudes, and habits that keep one self-contained and contribute to the delusion of not needing anything from outside the self, especially not from a loved one. (It is important, of course, to distinguish destructive forms of self-indulgence from positive self-interest, self-care, self-reflection, self-awareness, and compassion for yourself.) The presence of the fantasy bond can be inferred from the addictive use of tobacco, alcohol, or drugs, or from such unhealthy routines as excessively working, exercising, watching TV, shopping, or reading. Almost any behavior, if it becomes habitual, can be used to deaden feelings, with a negative impact on adult functioning and particularly on the ability to form and sustain a love relationship. Anything that promotes the self-indulgent orientation of the fantasy bond interferes with the gratification that comes from personal interactions.

Journal Exercise 5.1. Self-Soothing in Childhood and Self-Indulgence Today

Consider the following questions. As you answer them in your journal, elaborate with any other thoughts and ideas you may have on the topic. Your answers will help you identify your self-indulgent behavior.

- What are the ways I soothed myself as a young child? Did I suck my thumb? Twirl my hair? Anything else?

- Did I have a favorite item that I had with me all the time? Did I have a favorite blanket or stuffed animal? Anything else?

- Was there a ritual that helped me go to sleep? Did I rub a blanket? Suck my thumb? Anything else?

- Were there certain foods I liked because they comforted me? Did I like toast with butter? Noodles? Ice cream? Anything else?

- Was there a particular kind of behavior that calmed me down? Did I rock back and forth? Tap my fingers? Anything else?

- When I was growing up, did I develop any other self-soothing habits?

- As an adult, what are my self-indulgent habits?

- Am I addicted to any substances? What about alcohol? Nicotine? Drugs? Anything else?

- Am I self-indulgent around food?

- Do I ever engage in activities in a compulsive way? Work? Exercise? Shopping? Going online? Anything else?

- Do I ever use sex in an addictive, self-indulgent way? Do I masturbate excessively? Am I obsessed with internet porn? Anything else?

The Critical Inner Voice and the Fantasy Bond

Just as the critical inner voice supports other defenses, it upholds the fantasy bond. However, because the fantasy bond represents a primarily unconscious process, the critical inner voice does not comment on it directly. It doesn't say, *You should have a fantasy of being one with your parent.* Rather, it promotes the self-indulgent behavior that results from forming the fantasy bond. It encourages self-indulgent habits: *It's been a rough day—just go to bed.* It supports self-destructive behavior: *Have another cigarette! Have another drink! Go ahead and have another dessert!* It rationalizes compulsive habits: *You need to work hard! You really need to buy that outfit! You should binge-watch that show!* As people listen to the critical inner voice and engage in self-indulgent practices, they become progressively less invested in their relationships and the rest of their lives.

Journal Exercise 5.2. The Critical Inner Voice That Supports Self-Indulgence

Using your responses to journal exercise 5.1, think about a specific type of self-indulgent behavior that you engage in. Then follow the first four adapted steps of the Voice Therapy method.

1. *Identify* your thoughts about yourself in relation to your self-indulgent behavior you engage in today. For example, consider any thoughts that promote or justify this behavior. Write these thoughts down as "I" statements.

2. *Rewrite* your "I" statements as "you" statements in the form of attacks coming from your critical inner voice. Expand on them, continuing to rewrite them as "you" statements.

3. *Reflect* on what you have written, and record any new thoughts and insights.

4. *Confront* the attacks coming from your critical inner voice, using "I" statements to stand up for yourself.

Confronting Self-Indulgent Behavior

Although you can't directly confront the fantasy bond, because it's largely an unconscious defense, you can confront the behavior that sustains it, and you can defy the critical inner voice that encourages that behavior. You can challenge the self-indulgent habits that are manifestations of the fantasy bond and that interfere with your ability to establish intimacy with another person.

It is essential to confront the habits that you identify as self-indulgent, maladaptively self-gratifying, and dysfunctionally self-protective. These habits often include addictions and compulsive behavior. Disobeying the critical inner voice that encourages your destructive habits is vital to your ability to break them.

It is also advisable for you to control your subtler self-indulgent behavior. These forms of self-indulgence can include self-centered habits like expressing your irritation to waiters, pushing ahead of other people in line, or readily giving vent to your frustration when everything doesn't go exactly your way. The critical inner voice that drives this type of behavior tells you that you are being disrespected and taken advantage of. It's wise to ignore the critical inner voice that says, *This shouldn't be happening to you. You deserve to be treated better than this.*

Be aware of your negative attitudes, too. Are you overly concerned with your comfort? ("It's too hot!" or "It's too cold!") With your food? ("It has to be perfectly prepared!") With your possessions? ("I have to buy the best brand.") With your ailments? ("I think this head cold is turning into pneumonia.") With showing yourself a good time? ("I need to be having fun—I can't bear to be bored!") These prickly attitudes are representative of an inward focus that has a negative effect on relationships. Don't pay attention to the critical inner voice that makes you overly self-absorbed. Ignore it when it says, *Take care of yourself first* or *Make sure you've had a good meal* or *Make sure you're comfortable* or *Make sure you show yourself a good time!*

Another way to break into this self-contained system is to make a conscious effort to turn your focus outside yourself. Take action against the critical inner voice that influences you to tend exclusively to your own needs. Concentrate instead on the needs of others. When you feel for someone else and put that person's well-being and comfort ahead of your own, you're not just helping that person. You're also allowing yourself to benefit from the experience of feeling and expressing compassion and empathy. Being generous and helpful is also a natural, desirable way to relate to your partner.

Journal Exercise 5.3. Planning for Action Against the Critical Inner Voice That Supports Self-Indulgence

Using your responses to journal exercises 5.1 and 5.2, think about the self-indulgent behavior you uncovered, and about the critical inner voice that supports this behavior. Also think about what you said when you stood up for yourself and confronted your critical inner voice. Then, with these thoughts in mind, follow step 5 of Voice Therapy and *plan* the actions you will take to counter the critical inner voice that influences you to engage in self-indulgent behavior. Write these actions down, being detailed and specific about what you will do with respect to particular people, communication, behavior, situations, and so on. You will *implement* your plan in step 6 of Voice Therapy.

The Fantasy Bond in a Couple

Turning to someone else for love interrupts a person's self-indulgent habits and threatens other remnants of the original fantasy bond as well. As people develop a closer, more intimate relationship, they break out of their self-centered orientation, wanting their needs to be met by their partner and also desiring to meet their partner's needs. But this emotional give-and-take makes people feel vulnerable and unsafe. To relieve these feelings, many people unconsciously reestablish the fantasy bond, this time with their partner. Their real feelings of love and the delight they once took in interpersonal exchanges are slowly replaced by the fantasy of being merged with and magically connected to each other. They now have a fantasy of being one with their mate, just as they did with their parent in infancy and early childhood.

It is difficult to identify exactly when the fantasy bond is established in a relationship. The transition from real love to the fantasy of love is subtle and hard to detect. The fantasy bond can be inferred from certain types of behavior that show that the partners have moved away from actively relating and expressing love to one another. The changes described in the sections that follow are often signs that the fantasy bond has formed within a couple.

Form Replaces Substance

Couples caught up in the fantasy bond typically focus on form over substance. That is, they place more value on symbols of their union than on maintaining genuine intimacy in real time. They put great importance on honoring established routines, rituals, and traditions, such as birthdays, anniversaries, fixed date nights, and regular vacations. As long as these symbolic activities are maintained, the fantasy of love is upheld, regardless of whether the couple is actually emotionally close and loving. Both people begin operating more from habit and a sense of obligation than from choice. For example, Peter and Emily's focus on the traditions that characterized their family life helped them deny the painful reality of Peter's addiction and of how distant they had become from each other:

Peter and Emily had five children, and their life was marked by numerous family traditions. Among these were a summer camping trip, elaborate Thanksgiving and Christmas celebrations, and an annual blowout for their anniversary. The children's birthdays, graduations, and sports victories were also commemorated with lavish events. Everyone thought of Peter and Emily as the perfect couple and envied their family life.

However, the truth was radically different. After suffering a back injury twelve years earlier, Peter had become addicted to prescription pain medication. Emily ignored all the signs that her husband was an addict. As he became depressed and dysfunctional, her response was to be upbeat and try to cheer him up. At their annual family events, Emily acted lively and vivacious to cover for Peter's withdrawn behavior. At home, Peter was annoyed by Emily's Pollyannaish attitude, and she was irritated by his dark moods. They spent most of their time apart and were rarely sexual.

Finally, one of their children came home to visit and was alarmed to see the state Peter was in. He confronted his parents about his father's addiction, and even though Peter and Emily were both resistant to acknowledging the seriousness of their situation, their son's concern reached them, and they agreed to seek help.

Individuality Is Sacrificed

As the fantasy bond becomes stronger, both partners sacrifice more and more of their individuality in order to maintain the illusion of being one. They gradually assume an attitude of ownership over each other, with little concern for the partner as a separate person. Eventually each of them effectively disappears as a distinct human being.

As partners forfeit their independence, they become increasingly codependent (as opposed to interdependent). Both are weakened as individuals, and they lose sight of the reality that they are both capable of functioning on their own. Operating as half of a whole rather than as a complete person is slowly debilitating. When the individuals in a couple stop regarding themselves and the partner as separate beings, they are unable to see each other clearly. They become blind not only to the positive traits in the other but also to the other's negative or self-destructive qualities. With this limitation, they are no longer able to offer empathy and compassion and cannot be true friends to each other.

Equality Is Damaged

As partners give up their autonomy, the equality between them erodes. When they stop relating as two separate people, their relationship tends to become unbalanced and unequal. Often one person takes on the role of parent while the other assumes the role of child. In areas where one partner is weaker or less accomplished than the other, it is tempting for that partner to lean on the other and become progressively more dependent. This type of dependency further weakens people and they become more dysfunctional. If a partner is stronger or more capable in any way, there is a tendency for that partner to take over and assume control in the relationship. This authoritarian role disrespects one partner's capability and disregards the other's vulnerability. These polarizing postures don't just foster inequality and upset the balance in a relationship. They are also fundamentally dishonest because neither partner is a parent or a child; they are both simply adults. Consider Gretchen and Maggie, who relished the equality and companionship they felt at the beginning of their relationship but ended up acting out the roles of parent and child with each other:

Gretchen and Maggie had met when they were training for a marathon. Gretchen was an attorney, and Maggie was a trainer at a gym. Their friendship quickly grew, and they became romantically involved.

Gretchen was ambitious and driven. Maggie was fun-loving and carefree. Gretchen brought stability to Maggie's life, and Maggie helped Gretchen loosen up and not take everything so seriously. After six months, Maggie moved in with Gretchen.

Maggie wanted to start a private practice as a personal trainer, and Gretchen supported her so she could pursue her dream. This decision unexpectedly led to a serious decline in their relationship. Gretchen criticized Maggie for being disorganized and unfocused. Maggie resented Gretchen's superior attitude and rebelled against her suggestions. They began to have fights in which Gretchen would be parental and reprimand Maggie, and Maggie would react childishly. As they became more polarized, they began to talk about splitting up.

Sexuality Wanes

In general, the fantasy bond has a detrimental impact on sexual relating. Form and routine gradually replace lively and spontaneous sexual interactions. Each partner begins to relate as a mere extension of the other—an appendage—and they both become less appealing to each other; neither of them is any more attracted to the partner than to his or her own arm. Inequality between partners fosters a specific kind of hostility and resentment that can permeate the couple's sexual relationship. Typically, the partners are less and less frequently intimate, until they ultimately have just another sexless relationship.

People may also avoid physical intimacy and sexuality because a satisfying sexual experience can powerfully disrupt the illusion of connection provided by the fantasy bond. The sex act is a real but temporary physical connection that is followed by a distinct separation. Similarly, moments that are emotionally personal and intimate, with close and affectionate contact, always come to an end, at least for a time, as the partners move on with their everyday lives. Each type of transaction has an ending and necessitates a letting go. For these reasons, authentic love and sexual intimacy can challenge the fantasy of connection and arouse acute awareness of aloneness.

Communication Breaks Down

Formation of the fantasy bond usually leads to communication breakdown within a couple. When the partners' life together becomes more focused on the superficial aspects of their relationship, their conversation also becomes more superficial and practical. When they engage in behavior that is routine and predictable, they tend to seek comfort in discussion of the same narrow range of topics. When the partners sacrifice their individuality in order to relate as a unit, they often invade each other's boundaries. They may even speak for each other and treat each other disrespectfully. Each partner may become dismissive and impatient when the other talks or may not listen at all. When each partner no longer sees the other as who the other is, they both lose the ability to communicate the way they would with anyone else. Instead, they relate to each other with less compassion, empathy, interest, and understanding. Ellen and Bruce are an example of partners who were originally kind and respectful in their communication, but whose interactions gradually became tense and hostile:

> After Ellen and Bruce got married, they left their jobs to start a company together. As it prospered, they began speaking at business conferences and conventions. They became well known on the speaking circuit, and their seminars were well attended. They were inspiring speakers and role models to many in their trade.
>
> As Ellen and Bruce became caught up in the image of being a power couple, they began to lose sight of treating each other with kindness and respect. They became irritable and sarcastic with each other. When they were setting up their displays, Ellen snapped at Bruce. When they were giving instructions to the hotel staff, Bruce interrupted Ellen and talked over her. This pattern became the rule rather than the exception. It was hard for observers to reconcile the fact that these two hostile people were the same cheerful couple who appeared on the posters in the lobby.

Journal Exercise 5.4. Behavior That Indicates a Fantasy Bond

Consider the following questions. As you answer them in your journal, elaborate with any other thoughts and ideas you may have on the topic. Your answers will help you identify the behavior that indicates a fantasy bond.

- Are my partner and I not as close as we used to be? Are things somewhat distant between us?

- As a couple, have my partner and I become involved in routine behavior and activities?

- Are we spontaneous? Do we do things that are unplanned and in the moment? Do we ever do something just because it's what we feel like doing right now?

- As a couple, do we do things out of habit or obligation? Do we have an established date night, or do we always go out to the same restaurant? Do we always spend time with the same people?

- Have I stopped pursuing any independent interests?

- Has my partner stopped pursuing any independent interests?

- Are there ways I have subjugated myself to my partner?

- Am I more vocal and expressive of myself when I am away from my partner?

- Am I in the habit of thinking of myself as half of a couple rather than as an individual?

- Do I often begin a sentence with "we" when I could begin it with "I"?

- Have I stopped respecting my partner's boundaries? Do I tend to act as if what belongs to my partner belongs to me?

- Do I think my partner completes me? Do I regard my partner as my soul mate?

- Has the equality in my relationship gradually eroded?

- Has one of us taken on the role of child, with the other taking on the role of adult?

- Does one of us tend to act incompetent and unsure, and does the other act parental and authoritarian?

- When we relate, is one of us condescending and punishing, and is the other victimized and intimidated?

- Has the communication in my relationship deteriorated?

- Are our conversations mostly superficial and practical?

- Do we often speak for one another?

- Do we often interrupt each other?

- Do I ever act dismissive and uninterested when my partner is talking?

- Is there often an irritable or angry tone in our communications?

- Do I tend to make sarcastic or cynical remarks about my partner or our relationship?

- Are there now long periods of silence when neither of us seems to have anything to say?

- Has our lovemaking become dull and routine?

- Do we have less sex, and is it less passionate?

- Am I less spontaneous sexually?

- When we're sexual, am I less exploratory and expressive than I used to be?

- Am I less flirtatious than I used to be?

- Does a long time go by when we aren't sexual and I don't notice?

How the Critical Inner Voice Enables the Fantasy Bond

The critical inner voice supports behavior that is symptomatic of the fantasy bond by providing rationalizations and excuses and by placing blame on circumstances. This symptomatic behavior helps people deny reality and replace it with a fantasy. In the earlier example of Peter and Emily, the critical inner voice in each of them supported the idealization of their relationship by denying the truth about Peter's addiction and the impact it was having on them. Peter's critical inner voice said, *There's no problem here. You're not an addict. These are prescription meds that you're taking.* Emily's critical inner voice told her, *Everything's okay. Your family's still together and doing all the things you've always done. Everyone looks happy. Nothing's wrong.*

The critical inner voice can justify the sacrifice of your individuality in a relationship: *So you're a little quieter when he's around! Maybe you're just content and happy to be with him. You complete each other. He's the yang to your yin.* For Gretchen and Maggie, the critical inner voice in each of them rationalized their behavior and interfered with their being able to address the inequality that was hurting their relationship. Gretchen's critical inner voice said, *Maggie's so flaky! You have to watch her, or she won't get anything done.* Maggie's critical inner voice said, *Gretchen can be a nag, but she only does it because she cares about you.*

The critical inner voice can encourage you to withdraw sexually: *You don't have to be sexual tonight. He knows you love him. It doesn't mean anything that you're not sexual that often these days—you have reached a deeper level of love.* For Ellen and Bruce, the critical inner voice used the circumstances of their job to explain away the animosity that had developed between them: *He's not being mean to you. He's just irritated by the hotel staff* or *She's in a bad mood because of having trouble with the PowerPoint presentation.*

It is helpful to recognize that this type of critical inner voice operates as an enabler of the destructive behavior that maintains the fantasy bond in a relationship. It works the same way an enabler does in drug addiction and domestic abuse, making it possible for the addict or the victim to persist in self-destructive behavior and avoid the consequences. And just as an enabler does not have the best interests of the addict or victim in mind, the critical inner voice that excuses and justifies your destructive ways of relating does not have your best interests at heart.

Journal Exercise 5.5. Your Critical Inner Voice That Supports Behavior Indicating the Presence of the Fantasy Bond

Using your responses to journal exercise 5.4, think about possible indications of the fantasy bond in your relationship. Then follow the first four adapted steps of the Voice Therapy method.

1. *Identify* any thoughts you use to justify and rationalize behavior that indicates the presence of the fantasy bond in your relationship, using "I" statements. Write these statements down in your journal.

2. *Rewrite* your "I" statements as "you" statements in the form of encouragement from your critical inner voice for you to engage in this symptomatic behavior. Expand on them, continuing to rewrite them as "you" statements.

3. *Reflect* on what you have written, and record any new thoughts and insights.

4. *Confront* the destructive enablement coming from your critical inner voice, using "I" statements to stand up for yourself.

Challenging the Fantasy Bond in a Couple

A first step toward knowing that you're dealing with the fantasy bond is realizing that you are not as close to your partner as you used to be. Once you acknowledge this reality, it is easier to become aware of the various kinds of defensive behavior that are creating the distance. For instance, you can notice if you and your partner are having fewer personal conversations or spending less real time together or taking each other for granted. You can become aware of ways you have changed from how you were when your relationship began—for example, you may have fewer close friends or not as many personal interests as you used to. If you and your partner are alert to changes indicating that the fantasy bond has diminished your original closeness and the vitality of your relationship, you can both take action to recapture your closeness and vitality. The actions described in the sections that follow can help you challenge the fantasy bond.

Keep the Substance of Your Relationship

To keep your relationship real and fresh, you can resist taking a unique, in-the-moment experience with your partner and turning it into a regular routine. You can consciously avoid constructing your life and your relationship in a way that is so orderly and predictable that there is no room for spontaneity and surprise. You can make sure not to get caught up in everyday busyness to the point where you and your partner are living parallel lives rather than sharing your life together. You can make it a priority to spend time enjoying each other's company, having fun together, and getting involved in shared activities and interests. Most important, you can make a concentrated effort to slow down enough to get in touch with your feelings and communicate with each other from that feeling place. To return to Peter and Emily, who decided to deal with Peter's addiction, Emily's denial, and their mutual alienation, they worked hard to rebuild their trust and closeness:

> After their son exposed Peter's drug addiction, Emily and Peter had to face the fact that their life together was less than ideal. Peter went into a rehab program, and they both entered therapy, where they addressed the reality of their situation. When Emily dropped her role as family cheerleader, she experienced the pain of her real feelings. When Peter was honest about the extent of his addiction, he began to open up and feel the emotions that he had been trying to kill off with drugs.

They focused their efforts on Peter's sobriety and on reclaiming their relationship. With these goals in mind, they decided to take a break from their annual family events. They canceled their summer vacation, and Thanksgiving and Christmas became casual family gatherings. Instead of their usual anniversary party, the two of them went out to dinner alone. In therapy, they continued to tackle the issues that had developed between them over the years. Gradually, they were able to deconstruct their fantasy bond and rebuild a relationship characterized by honest relating.

Preserve Your Independence and Protect Your Partner's

As one partner in a couple, it is vital that you strive to maintain your own independence as well as to support the independence of your partner. You can actively pursue your own interests and aspirations, and you can encourage your partner's separate interests and aspirations. Maintaining an empathetic attitude toward your mate will help you react to your partner as a separate person and be attuned to your partner's distinctive personality. Maintaining your individuality will keep you and your partner from relating as a unit.

It is also important to be realistic, and to view yourself and your partner clearly—the strengths and good qualities along with the limitations and weaknesses. Resist the temptation to idealize your relationship. This aspect of the fantasy bond may seem positive, but in truth it disrespects the autonomy of both individuals. If you look at your relationship objectively, you can develop an appreciation of what it offers each of you and also of how it can be improved.

Support Equality in Your Relationship

You can strive to maintain equality in your relationship by taking responsibility for remaining an adult and not falling into patterns of relating unequally. You can identify the ways in which you are acting like a parent or a child with your partner, and you can make an effort to avoid slipping into that role. You can look for parental behavior or attitudes on your part. Do you act righteous, judgmental, or condescending toward your partner? Do you treat your partner like a child? Do you feel that you know better than your partner or are more capable? You can also investigate any childish behavior or attitudes on your part. Do you act like a victim, immature and powerless? Do you treat your partner like your parent? Do you want your partner to help you or look out for you or take care of you? Let's return to the example of Gretchen and Maggie, who decided not to separate but instead to rid their relationship of the parent-child dynamic that was threatening to ruin their love:

> For Gretchen and Maggie to reestablish equality in their relationship, each of them had to confront the unequal role she had taken on. Gretchen concentrated on controlling her tendency to take over and advise Maggie. Maggie focused on not being the irresponsible child; for instance, she began to set and then meet deadlines.
>
> Each of them had to stop listening to the critical inner voice that rationalized the other's unequal behavior. In their conversations, Gretchen spoke directly to Maggie, not as a disapproving, dismissive parent but as an equal adult. Maggie resisted the tendency to react childishly and made sure to listen and respond from an adult perspective. Both women sought to reestablish equality in their relationship by focusing on those aspects of their own behavior that were helping to create the disparity between them.

Sustain a Healthy, Interactive Sexuality

The same qualities that indicate good communication also indicate healthy sexuality within a couple—for example, making eye contact and being attuned to your partner. When you are vulnerable and open in your sexual interactions, you will experience deeper intimacy with your partner. Clearly state what you want, and express interest in what your partner wants. Freely indicate your desires. Free expression can involve explicit verbal statements as well as nonverbal cues, such as the physical posture you adopt and the way you move.

It is equally important to change any behavior that diminishes your sexual relationship. For example, if the sex act has become automatic and even mechanical for you, you can be more personal and engaged when making love. If you notice that you have been discouraging your partner from approaching you, you can be open and responsive to your partner's approach. It is also useful to identify and change addictive sexual habits, such as obsessive involvement with pornography or compulsive masturbation, because these activities diminish sexual intimacy. Combining sex with love provides the greatest intimacy and gratification. Sexuality is one of the most important aspects of a romantic relationship and can provide a deep sense of fulfillment in life.

Maintain Communication

Perhaps the most obvious indication of the fantasy bond's presence is deterioration in a couple's communication. Therefore, it is helpful to pay special attention to how you are talking with your partner. Notice if your conversations have degenerated into talk that is primarily about superficial, practical, or predictable topics. Avoid being impatient, irritable, or short with your partner. Don't be dismissive or sarcastic. Resist the temptation to speak for your partner, or as a couple. When Bruce and Ellen received some unexpected feedback, they were forced to notice that their style of communicating with each other had become abrasive, even hostile:

> Bruce and Ellen distributed an evaluation form after one of their seminars, and several participants commented on how nastily the two of them had behaved toward each other. A few participants even felt that the animosity between them had permeated the entire seminar. At first Bruce and Ellen were shocked, but then they realized that they needed to take a serious look at their behavior. They vowed to be respectful and kind in their interactions. When they were stressed or

under pressure, they made a conscious effort to treat each other decently. When anger arose between them, they addressed it directly in a reasonable discussion instead of making sarcastic remarks or hostile asides.

Think about how you are listening to your partner. Instead of interrupting, be attentive when your partner is speaking. Take an interest in what your partner is saying instead of just waiting impatiently for your turn to speak. Try to understand things from your partner's perspective.

Also notice what your body language is communicating to your partner. Your body language can actually be more significant than what you are saying with words. For example, when you say yes while slowly shaking your head no, you give a mixed message that creates confusion and distrust in your partner. Or when you say that you understand, but with an angry look on your face, your partner picks up your underlying anger.

You need to pay attention to subtle indications of the fantasy bond, too. Do you look at your partner while you're talking? Are you less affectionate than you used to be? Do the two of you no longer share amusing moments or laugh together? Are you spending more time apart?

Clearly, there is much to notice and be aware of if you want to preserve good communication with your partner. In fact, it's easier just to take each other for granted. But partners caught up in the fantasy bond often end up as two lonely people, coexisting and occupying the same space but rarely talking.

Journal Exercise 5.6. Planning for Action to Challenge the Fantasy Bond

Using your responses to journal exercise 5.5, think about the fantasy bond as it may be affecting your relationship, and about the critical inner voice that supports it. Also think about what you said when you stood up for yourself and confronted your critical inner voice. Then, with these thoughts in mind, follow step 5 of Voice Therapy and *plan* the actions you will take to counter the critical inner voice that influences you to form and maintain the fantasy bond. Write these actions down, being detailed and specific about what you will do with respect to particular people, communication, behavior, situations, and so on. You will *implement* your plan in step 6 of Voice Therapy.

Summary and a Look Ahead

The fantasy bond—the infant or young child's illusion of magical union with a parent or caregiver—eventually leads to a feeling of pseudoindependence in the older child, a feeling sustained by different kinds of self-soothing behavior. It persists into adulthood and is manifested in self-indulgent habits that seriously interfere with forming and maintaining good relationships. A new love relationship poses a threat to the orientation of self-containment, in which case a new fantasy bond is often established with the new partner. According to Erich Fromm (1956, 87), "There is only one proof for the presence of love: the depth of the relationship, and the aliveness and strength in each person concerned; this is the fruit by which love is recognized." But the presence of the fantasy bond in a couple seriously interferes with the partners' ability to sustain the vitality of their relationship. To preserve and protect the vitality of your love relationship, you need to challenge any and all elements of the fantasy bond between you and your partner. Being vigilant, breaking negative habits of relating to your partner, and withstanding the anxiety and discomfort of making those changes will also help you challenge a harmful by-product of your anti-self and the fantasy bond—your negative identity, described in the next chapter.

CHAPTER 6

When Love Challenges Our Negative Identity

We know what we are, but not what we may be.

—William Shakespeare, *Hamlet*

When we are loved and admired, there is often a discrepancy between this present-day reality and the way in which we are used to seeing ourselves. The disparity is subtle and not always obvious to us. Instead, it may show up in little suspicions we have: "Why's he smiling at me? I'm not pretty" or "Why does she want to be with me all the time? I'm not all that interesting" or "What's he see in me? I'm not so amazing." This chapter explains how being valued or seen in a positive light can be confusing because it goes against the negative self-concepts we formed while growing up. Being valued in this way contributes to a sense of psychological disequilibrium, which often causes us anxiety. We then react by rejecting the new identity of being valued and push love away. Some of the journal exercises in this chapter will help you recognize what your negative identity is and uncover the critical inner voice that supports it. Other exercises will assist you in planning actions to counter old ways of regarding yourself negatively. Still others will help you define your real identity and plan actions that accurately represent it.

Your Negative Identity

When we first fall in love, we have a positive response to feeling understood and valued by someone who matters to us. But eventually we can find ourselves faced with two opposing views of who we are: the familiar, albeit negative, view of ourselves that we have maintained most of our lives, and our loved one's new positive, objective view of us.

On an unconscious level, we are torn between these two views and don't know which one to believe. Even though our original self-image may have caused us a good deal of suffering, it is an identity we are used to and feel safe with, so we are reluctant to change it. A positive, more accurate self-image conflicts with our long-held concepts about ourselves and about reality and leaves us temporarily without a stable sense of who we are. As a result, we may try to avoid the dreaded loss of our identity and our security by rejecting our loved ones' affection for us and their acknowledgment of our positive qualities. Consider Calvin, whose negative identity of being a nerd was threatened when a woman at work developed a romantic interest in him:

> Calvin, a software programmer, was absorbed in his work. He was well liked for his warmth and quick wit, but his narrow circle of friends and limited social life made it difficult for him to meet someone he could develop a romantic relationship with. It didn't help that he became shy and awkward in the presence of women.
>
> When Elena joined Calvin's team, they spent long hours working together. Elena was attractive and lively. Since Calvin felt confident and relaxed in the work environment, he felt more himself and related easily, joking and even flirting with her.
>
> Elena found Calvin engaging and intelligent. As their project came to an end, she reached out to him and suggested that they go out for a drink after work. Suddenly Calvin felt nervous around her.
>
> At the restaurant, he was shy and unsure of what to talk about. He was distracted by thoughts that Elena was too

pretty for a nerd like him. Elena was confused: Did Calvin even like her? Had she been wrong to sense a spark between them?

How Your Negative Identity Developed

Our old identity is often negative. It is partly a by-product of the anti-self, as described in chapter 2, and partly a by-product of the fantasy bond, as described in chapter 5. This identity comes from our early family life and from any negative ways in which we were viewed, negative behavior we imitated, and negative ways in which we were treated.

Starting in infancy, children naturally assimilate the ways in which their parents see them. After all, our first image of ourselves comes from how we saw ourselves reflected in our parents' eyes. Unfortunately, however, parents don't always perceive their children accurately or completely. In fact, parents often attribute fixed identities to their offspring—"the good one," "the bad one," "the smart one," "the wild one," and so on. A negative identity can be created directly (for example, through actual comments or criticism) or indirectly (for example, through innuendo or negative comparisons to siblings or other kids). Even when an identity is created with kindly intent, as when special accommodations are made for a child who has been labeled "shy," "uncoordinated," or "a slow learner," the underlying message to the child is still negative.

Imitation is a powerful form of learning (Bandura 1975; Bandura & Walters 1963). Therefore, from the time they are very young, children model their parents' behavior, including their parents' negative habits and characteristics. Children automatically incorporate their parents' positive and negative traits as their own. The parents' positive habits and traits contribute to a child's developing feelings of self-worth and confidence, whereas the parents' negative habits and traits contribute to the child's negative identity. Even when children are able to discern parental habits and traits they do not like, they often take them on as parts of their own identity. Let's return to the example of Calvin:

Calvin's negative identity came from being labeled in certain ways by his parents—they bragged about his intelligence, but they often remarked that his interests were strange and that he was different from other boys, and they referred to his friends as "odd" and "nerdy." But Calvin's negative identity also came from how Calvin had modeled his father's behavior—Calvin's father was shy and diffident, and Calvin's physical awkwardness and social discomfort were an imitation of his father's demeanor.

Our negative identity is also a consequence of the fantasy bond and our primitive need to maintain a positive view of our parents. To sustain the illusion of unbroken and unbreakable attachment to their parents, children must obscure their parents' inadequacies; if these cannot be denied, then they represent a threat to the magical union between parent and child. For example, if a parent is so incompetent as to provoke anxiety in a child, the child preserves the fantasy bond with the parent by telling himself that he himself is the source of his anxiety. If a parent is emotionally hungry or intrusive, the child preserves the fantasy bond by coming to believe that she is inadequate because she can't satisfy her parent's demands. If parents are unable to respond to their children's needs and wants, the children preserve the fantasy bond by coming to view themselves as greedy and demanding. And if parents are physically abusive, their children cannot afford to see their parents as out of control or unduly harsh; instead, the children preserve the fantasy bond by imagining that they deserve punishment and abuse.

How Your Negative Identity Plays Out in Your Life Today

Once our negative identity is formed, we go on to elaborate on it and behave accordingly, thereby constantly reinforcing it. We tend to consider our negative identity as absolute and are generally unaware that it is only a label that was imposed on us, or an identity we took on, in childhood. Because we accept that our negative view of our-selves is simply the status quo, we rarely think of challenging it. In fact, if someone suggests a different reality, we often hang on to this remnant of the fantasy bond by stubbornly defending it. And when we do make a positive change in our self-image, we become anxious because the change marks a separation from our childhood self and the familial environment in which our self-image was formed.

As part of the original fantasy bond, we unconsciously continue to maintain an idealized image of our parents. We may be critical of them, even defiant and rebellious, but we are still protective of the idealization process that has been operating since we were young. Many of us would say that we have an objective view of our parents and our family, even a critical view, and yet we are still resistant to questioning the negative ways in which we were seen in our families; we're reluctant to recognize our parents' negative traits and averse to seeing that our parents treated us in ways that were hurtful to us.

Throughout our lives, our negative identity affects our responses to other people, especially those who love us and see us positively. We can be angry or even cruel when someone innocently contradicts our negative identity. Sadly, having this challenged often brings out the dark side of our personality. Jenna, for example, who had always regarded herself as a loner, was threatened when she fell in love with Matthew and wanted to have a baby with him:

> Jenna left home to travel around the world, a free spirit unencumbered by long-term emotional attachments. When she arrived in California, she met Matthew.
>
> Jenna had never imagined herself settling down or wanting to have children. But her casual friendship with Matthew grew into a serious involvement, and after a year and a half Jenna began wanting to have a baby with him. Matthew responded enthusiastically, and they talked about starting a family.
>
> Over the next months, Jenna became increasingly dissatisfied: Matthew wasn't exciting; he wasn't adventurous. She missed exploring the world. Her life was becoming boring

and routine. She began to dread the future—a baby would tie her down. She didn't really like children anyway.

She lashed out at Matthew, and they began fighting. By the end of the year, they were wondering if they should separate.

Journal Exercise 6.1. What Is Your Negative Identity Today?

Consider the following prompts. In your journal, answer the questions, and complete the partial statements with one or more words indicating a negative trait. As you do, write down any additional thoughts or insights that come to mind. Your responses will help you identify the negative ways in which you see yourself as an adult.

- I've always been …

- Ask anyone—they will tell you that I'm …

- I've come to accept that I'm …, and I'm okay with it.

- Are there positive ways that my partner sees me that I disagree with?

- What are the compliments that I tend to dismiss?

- Are there nice things my partner says about me that I consider exaggerations?

- Does my partner have positive views of me that, in my opinion, aren't at all justified?

- What are the nice things my partner thinks about me only because, as far as I'm concerned, my partner doesn't know the truth about me yet?

- Are there positive ways in which my partner sees me that are different from how I was seen as a child?

How the Critical Inner Voice Supports Your Negative Identity

The critical inner voice and its disparaging views reinforce a negative identity. The voice continues to support the negative ways in which you were seen as a child. For example, if you were labeled the "irresponsible" one, your critical inner voice may say, *You won't amount to anything. You mess up every opportunity that comes your way.* If you were the "chubby" one, your critical inner voice may say, *No matter what, you'll never be thin enough. And you'll never be attractive.* If you were the one who was seen as "not all that smart," your critical inner voice may say, *Just keep your opinions to yourself. Once you open your mouth, everyone will know how stupid you are.* The negative labels applied to you also imply unfavorable comparisons between you and other family members—unlike you, they are responsible, slim, smart, and so on—and these comparisons support your idealized image of these others.

The critical inner voice also attacks you for the negative qualities that you took on from you parents. For example, if you took on your father's irritability to avoid the reality that he was short-tempered, your critical inner voice may say, *Why can't you control your temper? You're the angriest one in this family.* If you had to cover up the truth about your mother's anxiety, your critical inner voice may say, *Why do you have to be so nervous about everything? You make everyone anxious!* Or your critical inner voice may rationalize and excuse your parents' behavior and qualities: *Don't blame your mother—she was under a lot of stress taking care of you kids* or *Even though your father punished you, he loved you and meant well.* Here is Calvin once again:

> Calvin used the steps of Voice Therapy to examine the critical inner voice that defined him as a nerd. First he considered the ways in which he had always thought about himself: *I've always been a nerd. That's just who I am. And that's how everyone has always seen me, and they can't all be wrong. And part of that is that I'm socially awkward. And I don't know how to relate to women. Especially pretty ones!*

Then he translated these thoughts into attacks by his critical inner voice: *You're a nerd. You've always been a nerd. Everyone knows that. Do you really think they could all be wrong? And look at you—you're so awkward with people! Especially women.* At this point, his critical inner voice attacked him about Elena: *You had no business going out with her. She's way out of your league. Are you insane?* The viciousness of these attacks made Calvin sad, which caused him to have compassion for himself. He challenged his critical inner voice: "I'm smart, but that doesn't make me a nerd. I grew up feeling that way, but it's not right. I wasn't a weird kid, and I'm not a weird adult. And I really don't think I'm awkward. My dad is awkward, but I have always had friends. If I weren't feeling like a nerd all the time, I'd be fine with women. I was totally myself with Elena when we were working. That's who I really am."

The critical inner voice continues to support the negative qualities that we assumed when our parents failed us. For example, if you took responsibility for a parent's emotional hunger, your critical inner voice may say, *You'll never be able to satisfy someone else's needs.* If you excused a parent for reacting to your needs and wants as intrusions, your critical inner voice may say, *You're too emotionally needy and demanding.* And if you explained away a parent's abusive behavior, your critical inner voice may say, *You're unlovable. You bring on the abusive treatment that you get.* Attacks like these by your critical inner voice perpetuate the blame that you assumed long ago for your parents' hurtful behavior and help you maintain your idealized image of them by clearing them of any wrongdoing. Let's check back in with Jenna:

Jenna also used the steps of Voice Therapy to investigate the critical inner voice that was undermining her relationship with Matthew. She uncovered vicious attacks directed at herself, at Matthew, and at her desire to have a baby.

She started by examining the critical inner voice that might be behind her sudden feeling of boredom and dissatisfaction with her life: *Your life is so routinized and mundane. What happened to your sense of adventure and curiosity about the world? Is this who you really are? Is this how you really want your life to be? It's all so dull!* She also looked into the critical inner voice that was fueling her criticism of Matthew: *This guy's a dud. He's not adventurous or interesting. He has nothing in common with you!* As Jenna continued to verbalize these attacks, the intensity of her anger took on the same tone and expression of her mother's anger toward her. She could hear her mother's voice: *And what happens when this relationship falls apart? You'll be stuck with the baby, just like I was stuck with you. This guy's going to abandon you, just like your father did me!* Jenna's critical inner voice became especially vicious when she explored her attitudes about having a baby. Once again, she heard her mother's voice: *Why do you want to have a baby? You don't even like kids. You think your life is boring now, just wait until you have a kid. It will tie you down and ruin your life. I know, because being stuck with you ruined my life. And what makes you think you will be a good mother? Didn't you learn anything from me? Being a mother sucks!*

Jenna was shocked by the cruelty of these attacks. She recognized them as representing her mother's attitudes, and she was angry when she confronted them: "What do you know about my life? You have no idea what it is to love a man and a child! All you know is how to avoid loving and caring about anybody. If I listened to you, I would be running all around the world, avoiding having any real relationships. My life is not boring. It is emotionally gratifying. And Matthew isn't boring, either. He is consistent and loving, but you call that boring. And the truth is that I am excited about having a baby with him. A baby isn't a burden! You treated me like a burden, but I wasn't. No child is." Standing up for herself left Jenna emotional, but afterward she felt relieved and loving and relaxed with Matthew.

Journal Exercise 6.2. Your Critical Inner Voice That Supports Your Negative Identity

Follow the first four adapted steps of the Voice Therapy method.

1. Using your responses to journal exercise 6.1, *identify* the negative thoughts about yourself that make up your negative identity. Write these thoughts down as "I" statements.

2. *Rewrite* your "I" statements as "you" statements in the form of attacks coming from your critical inner voice. Expand on them, continuing to rewrite them as "you" statements.

3. *Reflect* on what you have written, and record any new thoughts and insights.

4. *Confront* the attacks coming from your critical inner voice, using "I" statements to stand up for yourself.

How to Challenge Your Negative Identity and Maintain Your Real Identity

You can recover and maintain your real identity by taking actions that counter the critical inner voice supporting your negative identity. Taking these actions in your intimate relationship will help you align yourself with the positive view that your partner has of you instead of continuing to adhere to your familiar internalized view of yourself. To accomplish this goal, you can devise a plan of actions you can take that will represent your true identity. You can also identify actions you can stop because they represent your negative identity. It will probably feel unfamiliar and even peculiar at first to act in ways that express your real identity. Your critical inner voice will accuse you of being inauthentic. But if you ignore that voice and stay the course, you will become more comfortable with your real identity, and the attacks by your critical inner voice will subside.

Stop Doing Things That Promote Your Negative Identity

Once you have identified the voices that are promoting your negative identity and attacking your efforts to see and express your real self, you will have an idea of the actions you can take to support your true identity. For instance, if your old identity is that you aren't demonstrative, you can ignore the critical inner voice telling you that you are a cold person, and you can be affectionate with your partner. Recall Calvin's situation:

> Calvin planned actions that he could take to change his negative identity of being a nerd. Initially he was unclear about what to do. He worried that it would be phony of him to just start acting like someone he wasn't.
>
> But then he had the idea that he could stop talking about himself in negative ways. He would no longer make self-deprecating comments about being a geek. He wouldn't refer to his interests as strange or make jokes about not having a girlfriend.
>
> Implementing this idea was more difficult than he had thought it would be, because he hadn't been aware of how often he characterized himself as a nerd. He also decided to reach out to Elena for another date, but he chose an informal activity so he would be more relaxed and less self-conscious. They took a bike ride along the ocean, stopping at a beachfront café for a casual lunch. The rapport they had felt at work returned, and their relationship continued to develop.

Journal Exercise 6.3. Take Action Against Your Critical Inner Voice That Supports Your Negative Identity

Using your responses to journal exercises 6.1 and 6.2, think about your negative identity, and about the critical inner voice that supports it. Also think about what you said when you stood up for yourself and confronted your critical inner voice. Then, with these thoughts in mind, follow step 5 of Voice Therapy and *plan* the actions you will take to counter the critical inner voice that supports your negative identity. Write these actions down, being detailed and specific about what you will do with respect to particular people, communication, behavior, situations, and so on. You will *implement* your plan in step 6 of Voice Therapy.

Take a Realistic, Adult Perspective on Your Family

Another way to challenge your negative identity and see yourself realistically is to see your parents and your family system more accurately. Now that you're an adult, it is valuable for you to create a realistic narrative of your past and develop an understanding of your parents as real people, just like you. Creating this narrative and developing this understanding will dispel the idealized image of your parents that is left over from your childhood, and this will help you relinquish your negative identity.

Being loved gives you the opportunity to see your parents accurately because there is often a contrast between how you are regarded today and how you were treated as a child. Even though the difference between then and now represents a threat to your familiar idealization of your parents (R. W. Firestone & Catlett 1999), it also offers you a chance to perceive your parents and your childhood more realistically. Seeing your parents as real people will strengthen you. Today, in the present, you can accept the reality that your parents were limited in their ability to provide you with what you wanted or needed when you were young.

Jenna came to see that she was now an adult who could face the truth: severe depression had limited her mother's ability to provide the nurturance and care that a child needs.

Calvin came to see that his parents had been insensitive and wrong to label him a nerd. He no longer had to defend his father's image, could now feel compassion for this shy and awkward man, and was glad that he now felt differently about himself.

When you form a realistic image of your parents, you may feel visceral fear at the thought of losing what was once essential—your image of them as "perfect" parents. You may also feel subliminal guilt for symbolically abandoning your parents. But if you continue to formulate an accurate perception of your parents, both as they were in your childhood and as they are in your current life, your negative self-image will be diminished. To the degree that you can stop seeing your parents as flawless, you will stop regarding yourself as flawed.

Do Things That Promote Your Real Identity

Before you can create a plan of action to support your real identity, you have to clarify what your real identity is. Jenna's responses to her critical inner voice helped her come to know her real identity:

After her emotional response to the attacks by her critical inner voice, Jenna reflected on what she had said about herself and began to formulate what she valued and who she really was: "I value having love in my life, both the love of a man and the love of a child. I don't want to live my life alone, with no commitments. This is different from how I grew up, thinking about myself as a loner who was restless and on the move. This is different from the family I grew up in. I would never leave my family the way my father did, and I am not withdrawn and emotionally unavailable the way my mother was. I am a person who values maintaining meaningful relationships."

Journal Exercise 6.4. What Is Your Real Identity?

Consider the following prompts, and write your thoughts in your journal.

- Look back at journal exercise 6.2 and your answers to the critical inner voice that supports your negative identity. These answers are clues to what your real identity is. With these clues in mind, write down your thoughts and insights, and formulate a clear picture of your real identity.

- Complete the following statements, and write down any thoughts you have about your real identity.

  - I have always liked to...

  - One of the most meaningful things I've done in my life is ...

  - I have always been good at ...

  - I could spend hours ...

  - My best trait is that I'm ...

  - I value people who are ...

Once you know who you really are, what you must do to represent your true self becomes apparent to you. Let's turn once more to Jenna:

When Jenna articulated what was important to her, she knew what she wanted to do. Because her relationship with Matthew meant so much to her, she wanted to overcome the internal obstacles that were preventing her from having a committed relationship and a family with him. To accomplish this, she dedicated herself to working on herself in therapy and continuing to challenge her critical inner voice. And eight months later, she and Matthew happily announced that they were expecting a child.

Journal Exercise 6.5. Taking Action to Support Your Real Identity

- Using your responses to journal exercise 6.4, think about your real identity. Also think about what you said when you stood up for yourself and confronted your critical inner voice. Then, with these thoughts in mind, follow step 5 of Voice Therapy and *plan* the actions you will take to counter the critical inner voice and support your real identity. Write these actions down, being detailed and specific about what you will do with respect to particular people, communication, behavior, situations, and so on. You will *implement* your plan in step 6 of Voice Therapy.

- As a thought experiment, consider what happens when you see some positive quality in your partner but your partner disagrees with your perception. Don't you think you're right about your partner? So ask yourself this question: If you can be right about your partner, why can't your partner be right about you?

Summary and a Look Ahead

It is a sad fact that we react against love because it contradicts our negative beliefs about ourselves. We see ourselves as bad or terribly flawed, not as the basically decent human beings we are. Giving up our familiar self-image, however negative it may be, brings emotional upheaval because we feel threatened by the loss of our familiar, stable identity. We don't understand that our negative self-image may be a primary source of the alienation we feel in our romantic relationship. But if we challenge the critical inner voice that supports our outdated ways of seeing ourselves, we can live from a more realistic point of view. As we recover and express our real identity and free ourselves from the misperceptions of the past, we clear the way for more honest and intimate relating with those who are closest to us. And honesty and intimacy become more important than ever when love brings up feelings of guilt, the topic of the next chapter.

CHAPTER 7

When Love Triggers Guilt

I have a hard time convincing myself I'm worthy of being
happy.... Happiness shouldn't be associated with guilt.

—Jenny Lawson, blogger and author of
Let's Pretend This Never Happened,
You Are Here, and *Furiously Happy*

When we find ourselves sitting on top of the world and thinking that
life couldn't be better, we often become aware of someone we love or
care about who isn't doing as well as we are: "I'm so in love, but what
about Dad sitting alone in his apartment?" "What about Mom in her
unhappy marriage?" "What about my sister (brother, good friend,...)
who is struggling and unhappy?" Soon we start to sink, and before we
know it, guilt about having it so good has taken its toll. We have lost
our overall happiness, and the intimacy in our relationship is necessarily diminished.

The guilt being discussed in this chapter is not the obvious type
that we are all conscious of. It's not caused by other people's responses—
blatantly guilt-provoking attacks like "You're killing your mother" or
"You're ruining my life." Rather, this chapter focuses on the subtle,
largely unconscious guilt that comes from realizing that we are happier
than someone who is important to us. We most often feel this in relation to a close friend, a sibling, another significant family member, or

our family in general. We feel especially guilty about surpassing our parent of the same sex (Gilligan 1982; R. W. Firestone 1987; Lamb & Lewis 2004).

Some of the journal exercises in this chapter will help you recognize how you may be feeling guilty, and how your critical inner voice is supporting that guilt. The chapter also describes how we attempt to relieve our guilt for being happier than our family by re-creating our original family environment in our current relationship. Other journal exercises will allow you to identify the defenses you use to re-create your past and will then offer suggestions for confronting and counteracting those defenses with the Voice Therapy method.

Guilt for Being Happier and Different

We usually suffer the strongest guilt when we achieve more success in a particular area than our parent of the same sex. This is especially true when we develop a close and loving intimate relationship and our parent has an unhappy relationship. But we can also feel guilty if we develop friendships easily and our parent is lonely, or if we achieve financial success and our parent has monetary problems. We can also feel guilty about going beyond a brother, a sister, other family members, or close friends. For example, if a friend or a sibling is insecure or self-hating, we may attribute his or her emotional state to the fact of our good fortune, even if our friend or sibling is not directly jealous or envious of us.

When this type of guilt is aroused, we tend to imagine that our loved one's misery is exacerbated by our accomplishments and by the happiness in our lives. Our guilt in this situation can make us turn on ourselves and second-guess our own motives. We can come to feel that our personal goals are actually mean or destructive—that our motivation is to make someone else miserable rather than merely to pursue our own happiness. Whether this perception reflects reality or is completely imagined, when we sense that our actions are stirring up anxiety and animosity among family members or friends, we feel guilty and unconsciously rein ourselves in. In the following example, Sabrina's guilt in relation to her sister overshadowed her joy about her approaching wedding day:

> Sabrina and her younger sister, Natalia, were only a few years apart. In the games they played as children, Natalia was always the bride, and Sabrina happily took the role of member of the wedding party. Now Sabrina was getting married, and Natalia was happy for her and enjoyed helping plan the wedding. Nevertheless, Sabrina felt guilty because her sister was involved in a difficult relationship.
>
> As the wedding approached, Sabrina's humor became uncharacteristically self-deprecating. She belittled the wedding venue, ridiculed the decorations that were planned, and was critical of her appearance.
>
> Her brother noticed this and pulled her aside. As they spoke, Sabrina realized that she felt guilty that she was getting married and feeling so happy, whereas Natalia was talking about breaking up with her boyfriend.
>
> Sabrina didn't want to be distracted and worried about her sister during her wedding. She was motivated to correct her behavior because she wanted to fully experience this joyful moment in her life and share it with her husband.

When love leads us to change our old identity from childhood, as discussed in chapter 6, we invariably distinguish ourselves from our parents. Even though this distinction is positive, on a deeper level it can cause us trouble to feel that we are leaving someone behind who's been important to us. We feel guilt for being different and on our own, for standing apart from our family of origin as well as from other people who have been significant to us. If our interests, beliefs, or alliances differ from theirs, we can feel as though we are betraying a family allegiance.

We can also feel guilty in relation to our parents when love breaks into our childhood fantasy bond, as discussed in chapter 5. This dynamic often shows up as our guilt for not being the same as our parents. Children are the product of their parents' bodies, and children's own bodies are made up of their parents' DNA. This genetic sameness creates a biological chain that symbolically links the generations. But there's a hitch—this seemingly magical immortality can succeed only if children duplicate their parents' looks, character traits, behavior, or significant life choices. When we pursue priorities, interests, and goals that are different from those of our parents, we experience a form of survivor guilt because we disrupt the magical thinking that our parents will live on through us. We symbolically break the continuity between generations in our family constellation. In effect, we deny our parents a comforting illusion. This was clearly the case for Craig, who fell in love and was drawn to a lifestyle different from that of his parents:

> Craig was the only child of a hardworking couple with a successful family business. In high school, he had worked at his father's company during the summers. He enrolled at his father's college, where he joined his father's fraternity and was majoring in business. Essentially, he was being groomed to step in and take over for his father.
>
> But in his sophomore year, Craig took a class in global economics, and that was where he met Shelley. As he got to know her, he was inspired by her interest in Third World countries, and she exposed him to exciting ways of looking at the world.
>
> Craig's parents were upset when he quit the fraternity and moved in with Shelley. But they became angry when he changed his academic focus to international studies, with an emphasis on Third World countries.
>
> Craig was passionate and determined, but he was also racked with guilt, especially because he and Shelley were making plans to spend the summer doing volunteer work in an African country. He struggled with how to tell his parents that he was going abroad for the summer.

Journal Exercise 7.1. Guilt in Relation to Significant People

In your journal, answer the following questions, and write down any thoughts that come to mind.

- When I imagine myself being in a close relationship, do I tend to think of someone close to me who is unhappy about his or her love life? If so, who?

- When I am in a romantic relationship, is there someone I feel guilty in relation to? If so, who?

- Are my parents and siblings happy in their romantic relationships?

- Do I feel guilty in relation to any of them?

- Do most of my close friends and family members tend to be affectionate?

- Do they act romantic?

- Do my close friends and family members in long-term relationships still act as if they are in love?

- Do I feel self-conscious about being affectionate with my partner in front of any of them? If so, who?

- Do I play down my happiness when I'm with any of them? If so, who?

- Do I brush off acknowledgments about my romantic relationship around certain people? If so, who?

- Do I downplay my happiness in my relationship around certain people? If so, who?

How the Critical Inner Voice Encourages Guilt

The guilt generated by our being different from a parent or another influential person from our past, or by our having more success, joy, or love in our life than they do, can spark an escalation in the attacks coming from our critical inner voice. These attacks are usually not as obvious as *You're making your sister (brother, friend,...) look bad by comparison.* They are more subtle and are aimed at weakening our confidence and undermining our achievements. The critical inner voice tries to impair our success at work: *You're not smart enough for that position. You don't deserve that promotion. You won't be able to perform in this new job.* It tries to diminish love: *You lucked out in this relationship—you're not worthy of someone so nice. You sure have your partner fooled.* This escalation leads to the letdown we often experience after achieving happiness or an unusual success.

> Sabrina's critical inner voice attacked her and her wedding plans in order to diminish her happiness and relieve the guilt she felt in relation to her sister: *Your dress looks ridiculous. You should have lost weight for the wedding. This venue is pathetic—it looks cheap.* Then her critical inner voice became more direct: *Look at your sister! Her life is a mess, and here you are, being all thrilled! You're rubbing her nose in it. You're so cruel!* When Sabrina addressed these attacks, she confronted her guilt: "There's nothing wrong with me or my wedding. I am thrilled. And my happiness has nothing to do with anyone else's life. I wish the best for Natalia, as she does for me. And I'm not going to give this up just because of what you're telling me."

> From the beginning, Craig's critical inner voice attacked him directly and mirrored his parents' anger for causing them misery: *You are destroying your parents' lives and their future. They've been counting on you to keep their business going. You are so selfish, just thinking of yourself and what you want!* Craig confronted these attacks: "It is not my intention to hurt them.

I am sorry to mess up their plans, but I have to create my own life. I have to do what's right for me." Craig's critical inner voice also attacked Shelley: *This girl has turned your head and is ruining your life. She's turned you into some kind of bleeding heart!* In response, Craig said, "I love Shelley, and I'm grateful for the world she's opened up to me. But this is my passion as much as it is hers. And I feel lucky to have someone to share it with." His critical inner voice then bombarded him about his plans for the summer: *This is taking it too far. You are abandoning your parents! You don't give one damn about them.* Craig replied, "I love my parents and am grateful for everything they have given me. But this has nothing to do with them. It has to do with me and what I am passionate about, and with my love for Shelley."

Journal Exercise 7.2. Your Critical Inner Voice That Encourages Guilt

Follow the first four adapted steps of the Voice Therapy method.

1. Using your responses to journal exercise 7.1, *identify* your thoughts about someone you feel guilty in relation to, especially when your love life is good. Write these thoughts down as "I" statements, describing how you make this person unhappy.

2. *Rewrite* your "I" statements as "you" statements in the form of attacks coming from your critical inner voice. Expand on them, continuing to rewrite them as "you" statements.

3. *Reflect* on what you have written, and record any new thoughts and insights.

4. *Confront* the attacks coming from your critical inner voice, using "I" statements to stand up for yourself.

Taking Action to Overcome Guilt

What's the best way to overcome guilt? Don't give in to it! That sounds simple, but it's hard. Voice Therapy is helpful because confronting your critical inner voice strengthens your position and clarifies the actions you need to take. For example, Sabrina challenged and then ignored the critical inner voice that was criticizing her wedding plans and accusing her of hurting her sister, and she was able to enjoy her wedding day. And when Craig confronted the critical inner voice that was making him feel guilty about his parents' discomfort, he stopped turning against himself, took pride in his chosen field of study and his relationship with Shelley, and continued to speak openly about himself and his partner in a forthright and honest manner.

If you notice yourself feeling guilty, take a moment to think about what your critical inner voice is telling you, and then confront it. This will make it easier for you to stand your ground, honor your own choices, and enjoy your good fortune, even though doing so arouses your guilt. When you make a conscious effort to withstand the guilt you feel for being different or more successful than someone who has been important to you, you can become accustomed to your good fortune.

Journal Exercise 7.3. Taking Action Against Your Critical Inner Voice That Encourages Guilt

Using your responses to journal exercise 7.2, think about the person you feel guilty in relation to, and about the critical inner voice that supports this feeling. Also think about what you said when you stood up for yourself and confronted your critical inner voice. Then, with these thoughts in mind, follow step 5 of Voice Therapy and *plan* the actions you will take to counter the critical inner voice that encourages guilt. Write these actions down, being detailed and specific about what you will do with respect to particular people, communication, behavior, situations, and so on. You will *implement* your plan in step 6 of Voice Therapy.

Defensive Strategies: Selection, Distortion, and Provocation

When love comes along, and our newfound happiness makes us feel guilty in relation to a family member or someone else important to us, we often react quickly in self-defeating ways, and usually without being aware of what we are doing. We hold ourselves back and limit ourselves in order to eradicate the distinction that has been created by our happiness. No matter what has triggered our guilt, we often seek to relieve it by abandoning our course, making a U-turn, and going back to what was familiar before happiness appeared. Essentially, we return to being the person we used to be, and that usually means going back to who we were in our family of origin. One way to accomplish this U-turn is to introduce the psychological environment of our past into our present-day relationship, using three primary defensive strategies: *selection*, *distortion*, and *provocation*. These strategies are discrete but often work together.

Selection

If you select a partner who is similar to one of your parents, or to someone else who played a primary role in your childhood, there is little difference between your new relationship and the old one. How you are treated, seen, and related to will be consistent with what you experienced when you were younger. Keeping everything the same ensures that you will not feel the anxiety, fear, and guilt that can accompany your becoming an individual and distinguishing yourself from your family of origin or other early environment. You are able to maintain your sense of safety, security, and stability—but at a cost, as Maria discovered:

> Maria had a prestigious job in the tech industry. She was proud of her success and valued her independence. Maria's career differentiated her from her stay-at-home mom, who had assumed a submissive role in her marriage.

In her personal relationships, too, Maria was unlike her mother; she was confident and outgoing. As a single woman, she had been popular and dated fun-loving boyfriends.

But then she married Paul, who was stern and somewhat condescending. Over time, Maria's friends began to see a change in her. She was losing her old self-confidence and assertiveness, and she was deferring to her husband. In fact, she had chosen a man who related to her in much the same way that her father related to her mother, and to her.

Distortion

If your partner relates to you more positively than members of your family did, you can erase that contrast by distorting your partner and seeing him or her as having negative characteristics similar to those of your parent or other significant relative. For example, you may imagine disapproval, disinterest, or hostility where there is none. When you treat these distortions as though they are real, you are once again in familiar relationship territory. You may not be happy, but at least you are no longer anxious or guilty.

Even though Maria's husband was serious and could be uptight, he was also warm and did have an easygoing side. Paul loved Maria and seldom felt critical of her. But when he sometimes wore a pensive expression, Maria would misinterpret it as disapproval. She felt hurt by the perceived criticism, and then contrite. When this happened, Paul became confused by Maria's change in mood, and by her apologetic behavior toward him.

Provocation

Provocation is another defensive strategy you can use to re-create the psychological environment of your past. For example, if you were disregarded in your family, you can act in ways that elicit a dismissive response from your partner. If you were condescended to, you can be incompetent and childish and draw a parental response from your partner. When this occurs, your partner often ends up actually making the same kinds of judgmental and critical comments you heard as a child. In effect, you have turned your loved one into someone from your past.

At times Maria provoked Paul into taking a parental role with her. For example, although she had a good sense of direction, she would not know where she was and where she was going, or she would seem mystified by their finances even though she was in fact a good money manager. At these times Maria acted inept and helpless, and Paul became frustrated at having to direct her through the simplest tasks. He didn't like being put into the role of an authoritarian parent.

Journal Exercise 7.4. How You Re-Create Your Past in Your Current Relationship

In your journal, answer the following questions, and write down any thoughts that come to mind.

- What's the negative trait that I'm most critical of in my partner?

- Did anyone from my past have that trait?

- What negative trait was I or am I most critical of in my father? In my mother?

- Is there a similarity between what I see as my partner's most negative trait and what I saw or see as my father's or my mother's most negative trait?

- Has my view of my partner gone from being mostly positive to mostly negative?

- If so, what used to be my positive feelings? What were the traits I loved about my partner?

- What are my negative feelings now? What are the negative ways in which I currently see my partner?

- Did a significant person in my childhood have the same negative qualities?

- When do I overreact to my partner? What are the dynamics of those situations?

- Were there similar dynamics in my childhood that I reacted to strongly?

- If so, could it be that I am distorting my partner and either imagining or exaggerating my partner's negative qualities in order to re-create my past?

- With the preceding questions in mind, if I realize that my relationship has changed for the worse, is it possible that I am provoking this negative outcome in some way?

- Do I provoke parental reactions in my partner by being childish?

- Is my partner frightened and meek because I act angry and intimidating?

- Do I act irresponsible and draw judgmental responses from my partner?

- Do the dynamics between my partner and me replicate any family dynamics I grew up with?

Identifying and Challenging the Critical Inner Voice That Supports Selection, Distortion, and Provocation

Your critical inner voice supports and rationalizes the defensive strategies of selection, distortion and provocation. It reintroduces your original family dynamic into your current relationship by reinforcing your old identity and ensuring that your emotional environment is the same as it has always been.

Maria had subconsciously selected Paul to replicate the patriarchal structure of her parents' relationship and her family of origin. Her critical inner voice supported that choice by building Paul up to seem superior to her: *He knows so much more than you do! He's more experienced than you are.* At other times her critical inner voice left her feeling incompetent: *You don't know what you're doing. You would never be able to function without Paul.* It also distorted Paul by convincing Maria that he was judging her: *He thinks you can't do that. He thinks you're incompetent.* It encouraged the childishness in Maria that provoked Paul to become authoritarian and parental: *You're not smart enough to figure that out. You have to get him to help you.* Then, when Paul became irritated, Maria's critical inner voice said, *See? He really is critical of you. Besides, he's an angry, judgmental person.*

Voice Therapy can be used to plan and implement actions to counteract these defensive strategies. Once you have addressed the critical inner voice that is fueling these strategies, you will have an idea of the actions you can take to reduce your use of them:

Maria knew that her challenge was to relate to Paul as an equal, thereby establishing a relationship with him that was different from her mother's relationship with Maria's father. She decided she would stop herself from habitually deferring to Paul. She would ignore the critical inner voice telling her that she was incompetent, and she would start making decisions. She would actively challenge her misperceptions, which were based on her childhood experiences, and would stop viewing Paul as a judgmental parent and herself as an inept child.

Journal Exercise 7.5. Your Critical Inner Voice That Influences You to Reproduce Your Past in Your Current Relationship

Using your responses to journal exercise 7.4, think of a way in which you are repeating negative relationship dynamics from your past through selection, distortion, provocation, or a combination of these defensive strategies. Then follow the first four adapted steps of the Voice Therapy method.

1. *Identify* your critical thoughts about yourself in relation to repeating negative dynamics from the past, using "I" statements. Write these statements down in your journal.

2. *Rewrite* your "I" statements as "you" statements in the form of attacks coming from your critical inner voice. Expand on them, continuing to rewrite them as "you" statements.

3. *Reflect* on what you have written, and record any new thoughts and insights.

4. *Confront* the attacks coming from your critical inner voice, using "I" statements to stand up for yourself.

Journal Exercise 7.6. Taking Action Against the Critical Inner Voice That Influences You to Reproduce Your Past in Your Current Relationship

Using your responses to journal exercises 7.4 and 7.5, think about how you reproduce your past in your current relationship, and about the critical inner voice that supports this behavior. Also think about what you said when you stood up for yourself and confronted your critical inner voice. Then, with these thoughts in mind, follow step 5 of Voice Therapy and *plan* the actions you will take to counter the critical inner voice that influences you to repeat negative relationship dynamics from the past. Write these actions down, being detailed and specific about what you will do with respect to particular people, communication, behavior, situations, and so on. You will *implement* your plan in step 6 of Voice Therapy.

Summary and a Look Ahead

We often feel guilty when we have more happiness, love, or success in our lives than a particular parent, another significant family member, or a close friend. But we can use the Voice Therapy method to resist the critical inner voice that urges us to relieve our guilt by neutralizing the love in our present-day relationship. We can also become aware of our unconscious ways of reestablishing our past in the present, and then we can challenge that behavior. The Scottish psychiatrist R. D. Laing distinguishes between true and false guilt: "True guilt is guilt at the obligation one owes to oneself to be oneself. False guilt is guilt felt at not being what other people feel one ought to be or assume that one is" (Laing 1971, 152). Laing's distinction is especially relevant when it comes to love, and it makes our choices clear: we can base our behavior and our course of action on others' expectations and betray ourselves, or we can sweat out the guilt and anxiety that come with choosing our own destiny and remain true to ourselves. The latter choice will leave us more likely to be gratified in our relationships, more at peace with ourselves, and more prepared to deal with the profound sadness that love can arouse in us, as we'll see in the next chapter.

CHAPTER 8

When Love Arouses Deep Sadness

Joy's smile is much closer to tears than it is to laughter.

—Victor Hugo, *Hernani*

We often retreat from love when it unconsciously arouses painful feelings of sadness. This is not the kind of sadness that comes when our feelings are hurt or our heart is broken. That sadness makes sense to us. This type of sadness is perplexing because it is aroused when we are treated with kindness and compassion and sensitivity. One of the reasons it is difficult to understand these sources of sadness is that we expect love to make us happy.

When, in spite of being in love, we feel sad, this feeling may confuse us because it is counterintuitive. It is much easier to understand the sadness that is aroused by unhappy or negative events. Even though we may have difficulty understanding the sadness that comes from positive and loving experiences, if we really think about it, we are all aware of times we have known this feeling. It's the emotion you observe between a bride and groom when they tear up as they stand at the altar. It's the emotion you, as a member of the wedding party, experience as you witness them. It's the sadness that you feel when someone does something for you that indicates a special sensitivity to you. It's the sadness that surprises you when you do something for someone else that expresses your sensitivity toward them. It's the feeling that wells up inside you when you see somebody overcome a significant obstacle to their development or achieve a meaningful victory.

Sadness is generally misunderstood. When sadness is associated with unhappiness and emotional pain, it is an unpleasant experience, although even then it is a healthy release. Childhood is filled with this type of sadness because children are so often overlooked, misunderstood, and inadvertently hurt in the course of growing up. But there is more to sadness than unhappiness, and it is in our interest to broaden our understanding of an emotion that is typically considered negative.

This chapter will help you understand this paradoxical reaction to love by exploring where this sadness is coming from. It explains different ways in which we try to eliminate this feeling, and it offers suggestions for allowing yourself to feel sad. The chapter's journal exercises will help you examine your reactions to sadness, enabling you to identify the critical inner voice that promotes attitudes and behavior that discourage sadness and suggesting actions that will support your feeling sadness. Welcoming the sadness that comes from love allows for an even deeper closeness and special tenderness with your partner.

Where Does the Sadness in Love Come From?

The sadness aroused by love comes from two sources. One source is our long-buried pain. The other source is emotional closeness and intimacy that we experience in the present. An understanding of both sources helps explain how positive and rewarding interactions can precipitate sad feelings that we unconsciously try to avoid by rejecting or distancing ourselves from our loved one.

Sadness from the Past

To the degree that we have suffered a painful childhood, being treated with love and tenderness can cause us to be deeply saddened. In part, being responded to in this different way initiates our becoming aware of what we were missing as children. The contrast between the two kinds of treatment stirs up painful feelings of loss or rejection that we have suppressed, and we unconsciously expect these emotions to resurface with their original intensity. They don't, because we're adults now, not children. But we still reflexively react against feeling sad, and we often defend ourselves by pushing away the love that is triggering our sadness.

Sadness in the Present

At times of exceptional closeness with our partner, both of us are likely to feel sadness. This unexpected emotional reaction to love is quite common. Sadness is often aroused when we are open and vulnerable to each other, when we have a moving personal dialogue, and when we experience compassion and empathy for and from each other. During these poignant moments of communion, each of us has an appreciation of the preciousness of life. The love we are sharing enhances our existence and adds value to our life together. Consider the example of Oliver:

> Oliver had grown up distrustful of relationships, expecting that eventually he would get hurt. His parents had gone through a long and messy divorce when Oliver was a child, and afterward he had lived with his mother, who was bitter and depressed and never remarried. Oliver had experienced a few short-term involvements, but they ended badly.
>
> In therapy, Oliver investigated the parallel between the circumstances of his parents' marriage and his own inability to form a close relationship. He gained insight into how all his involvements had confirmed his distrustful feelings about love.
>
> After a year of therapy, Oliver met Dom, who was unlike the other men he'd been involved with. Dom was warm and acknowledging. He was open and easy to talk to. Oliver and Dom genuinely enjoyed each other's company, and Oliver felt at peace in their relationship.
>
> One evening Dom made dinner for them at his place, and Oliver was particularly touched by Dom's relaxed affection

and simple kindnesses. Later that night, Oliver reflected on how loving Dom had been to him, and he felt sad. He realized that he trusted Dom.

Sadness is perhaps most bewildering when it follows an especially intimate and gratifying sexual encounter. The combination of satisfying sex and emotional intimacy can elicit many different feelings—tenderness, excitement, pleasure in meeting the wants and needs of your partner, the thrill of having your own wants and needs met, and the gratification and joy that come from sharing such a meaningful experience. When eyes-open emotional intimacy is combined with passionate sex, two people are at their most vulnerable and accessible, and the sense of togetherness that follows often leaves them feeling sad.

Journal Exercise 8.1. Your Reactions to Sadness

In your journal, answer the following questions, and write down any thoughts that come to mind.

- Do I ever try not to cry? Do I try to hold back my tears?

- Am I ashamed or embarrassed if I feel sad? Do I apologize for crying?

- Do I look away when someone else is crying? Do I feel uncomfortable in their presence?

- Do I feel impatient with them? Do I wish they would pull themselves together or get a grip?

- Have I ever ridiculed someone for crying? When I was young, did I call other kids "crybaby"?

- When someone is crying, do I think the best thing to do is to help them stop?

- Do I try to make a joke or otherwise change the subject?

- Is there any behavior that I enlist to numb my own sadness?

- When I start to feel sad, do I reach for a cigarette or a drink?

- Do I go off by myself or engage in an activity that cuts me off from my sad feelings?

- Do I cry easily and often, or do I rarely cry?

- When was the last time I cried?

- Was I with someone or was I by myself?

- How did I feel afterward? Was I shaken up? Did I feel relief?

- What was the last movie or book that made me cry? What in the story made me sad?

- When was the last time I was with someone and we felt sad together? What were the circumstances?

- How did I feel afterward? Did I feel embarrassed and later avoid the person I had been with? Did I feel vulnerable and closer to that person?

- Has being kind to someone else, especially my partner, ever aroused sadness in me?

- Have I ever felt sad when someone, especially my partner, reached out to me in a way that was especially kind and sensitive?

- Do I feel comfortable feeling sad in front of my partner?

- Do I feel comfortable when my partner expresses sadness?

How We Cut Off Sadness

We cut off sadness with the same defenses we developed to cut off pain in our childhood—for instance, by isolating ourselves and withdrawing from interactions with others. We often resort to addictive behavior in an effort to dull our sadness. Alcohol, cigarettes, and recreational or prescription drugs are obvious, albeit temporary, ways to numb ourselves and escape from sadness, pain, and anxiety. So are eating and being sexual, which are both pleasurable undertakings that we can abuse in an effort to escape our unpleasant emotions.

As noted in chapter 5, everyday interests and routines can serve as addictions if we engage in them compulsively. Almost any activity, carried to an extreme, can cut us off from our feelings. But the gratification that comes from addictive behavior is short-lived, and the behavior must be repeated more and more often to continue providing the relief we seek. Oliver, for example, distracted himself from his sadness (and his closeness with Dom) by becoming engrossed in work:

> Oliver was self-employed, working from home on his blog, which had become popular and profitable. He was aware that he had a tendency to overwork and lose himself in writing, maintaining, and promoting the blog.
>
> During the week after his dinner with Dom, he threw himself into creating new blog content. Dom called Oliver a few days later, but Oliver said he was too busy to get together. All week, Oliver hardly communicated with Dom.
>
> When Dom stopped by over the weekend, Oliver barely looked up from his computer. Dom asked Oliver if he wanted to be left alone, and that was when something clicked for Oliver. He asked himself what he was doing. Was he so consumed by work that there was no room for his feelings for Dom or their developing relationship?

Journal Exercise 8.2. Your Behavior That Cuts Off Sadness

Read the following list, and identify any behavior you engage in to avoid sadness as well as other unpleasant feelings. In your journal, write down your thoughts about that behavior. For example, when and why did it start? When does it occur in your life today? How do you feel if you imagine stopping this behavior?

- Abusing alcohol

- Abusing prescription or recreational drugs

- Smoking cigarettes

- Overeating, or bingeing and purging

- Self-harming behavior, such as cutting

- Sex addiction

- Binge-watching TV or movies

- Playing video games for hours

- Mindlessly browsing the internet

- Nonstop reading

- Obsessive shopping

- Extreme and extensive exercising

- Overworking

If you engage in any addictive behavior that isn't on the preceding list, note it, and journal about it.

The Critical Inner Voice and Addictive Behavior

Our critical inner voice supports the various kinds of defensive behavior we use to cut off sadness and create emotional distance. One of the most destructive functions of the critical inner voice is its role in the cycle of addiction. It tempts us to use drugs, alcohol, or cigarettes for relief from sadness, pain, and anxiety. It encourages us to overindulge in normally gratifying activities, such as eating and having sex. It influences us to be compulsively involved in an everyday activity or routine. And then, after we've succumbed to its dictates, our critical inner voice turns on us and attacks us for being weak and easily corrupted. For example, Oliver's critical inner voice drove him to overwork and then attacked him for pulling away from Dom:

> Oliver tried to uncover the critical inner voice behind his sudden motivation to overwork. He had been unaware that his critical inner voice was what was driving him, but when he thought about the situation, he identified the voice's words, and its tone: *You'd better get to work! You're so caught up in this relationship that you've neglected your blog. There's a lot to do!* He realized that his critical inner voice was now attacking him for pulling away from Dom: *And now you've neglected Dom. You have no tolerance for closeness. You can't maintain a relationship. You're not cut out for this kind of thing.* Oliver answered these attacks: "First of all, I've been balancing my work and my personal life successfully. I'm not behind on a deadline or under any pressure with my blog. The real reason I put so much emphasis on working this week was to lose myself. And I can see that all of this was to kill those feelings I had about Dom the other night. So back off, and don't attack me for that. It's a challenge for me to be in a relationship like this, and I am definitely developing. But I have compassion for myself. It takes time."

Journal Exercise 8.3. The Critical Inner Voice That Encourages Addictive Behavior, Part 1

Think of some type of addictive behavior you may be using to cut yourself off from sadness or other difficult emotions. Then follow the first four adapted steps of the Voice Therapy method (steps 1 and 2 deal with the critical inner voice that influences you to engage in addictive behavior).

1. *Identify* the thoughts you use to justify and rationalize your behavior, using "I" statements. Write these statements down in your journal.

2. *Rewrite* your "I" statements as "you" statements in the form of directives coming from your critical inner voice that urges you to engage in this self-destructive behavior. Expand on them, continuing to rewrite them as "you" statements.

3. *Reflect* on what you have written, and record any new thoughts and insights.

4. *Confront* the directives coming from your critical inner voice, using "I" statements to stand up for yourself.

Journal Exercise 8.4. The Critical Inner Voice That Encourages Addictive Behavior, Part 2

Continue thinking about the same addictive behavior you examined in journal exercise 8.3. Then follow the first four adapted steps of the Voice Therapy method (steps 1 and 2 deal with the critical inner voice that attacks you after you have succumbed to its directives).

1. *Identify* your self-hating, self-punishing thoughts in relation to addictive behavior, using "I" statements to describe why you feel hateful or punishing toward yourself. Write these statements down in your journal.

2. *Rewrite* your "I" statements as "you" statements in the form of attacks coming from your critical inner voice. Expand on them, continuing to rewrite them as "you" statements.

3. *Reflect* on what you have written, and record any new thoughts and insights.

4. *Confront* the attacks coming from your critical inner voice, using "I" statements to stand up for yourself.

Misconceptions About Sadness

The critical inner voice has a lot to say about sadness in general, and what it has to say also applies to the sadness that comes from being loved. In fact, the critical inner voice interferes with our sadness, and then its interference inhibits our ability to be intimate with our partner.

The critical inner voice warns us that if we feel sad, we will be opening the floodgates. It tells us that sadness is abnormal and bad for us—that once sadness starts, it won't ever stop, and that sadness and depression are the same thing. The critical inner voice endorses what many of us heard growing up: "Don't be a crybaby! Crying is for sissies! You're falling apart—get it together! Nobody wants to be around a sad sack. Now, quit crying, or I'll give you something to cry about!"

As always, however, the critical inner voice is wrong, and it offers destructive advice. It also makes specific attacks on sadness, and many of us accept what it says as the truth. It is valuable for us to investigate our assumptions and misconceptions and examine the facts. What we discover will give us what we need to confront these attacks:

- The critical inner voice says, *Sadness is an abnormal emotion.* On the contrary; to be sad is to be human. In 1980, psychologist and researcher Robert Plutchik developed one of the most influential classification approaches for general emotional responses. Sadness is one of the eight primary emotions he identified (the others being anger, fear, disgust, surprise, anticipation, trust, and joy). He proposed that these "basic" emotions are biologically primitive and have a high survival value (Plutchik 2000). Sadness is not only a fundamental part of our being human; it plays a primary role in our survival as well.

- The critical inner voice says, *Sadness is bad for you.* And yet sadness is a natural state of mind that exists not only in humans but also in nonhuman primates, for good evolutionary reasons. It is beneficial for you to feel sadness. Many people resist feeling sadness because they anticipate being engulfed in a negative emotion. But when sadness is suppressed, it can build up so that when it is finally released, it is felt intensely. If sadness is felt as a natural part of everyday life, however, it arises and then departs, even when it is strongly felt. And there is great relief in letting it out. After expressing deep feelings of sadness, people report that they feel more unified or integrated and have a stronger sense of identity. In his book *Emotion-Focused Therapy*, Leslie Greenberg (2002, 303) observes, "Sadness of this type gives meaning to life and leaves us in some unique way feeling both invigorated and tired, maybe from the intensity of it all."

- The critical inner voice says, *Sadness is the same as depression.* It's true that we often equate sadness with depression, thinking of depression as an extreme state of sadness. And some of the same reactions (crying, lack of energy, grieving) occur in both of these emotional states, but the two are quite different from each other. Sadness is a healthy human emotion, a natural reaction to painful or even unusually positive circumstances. Everyone experiences sadness. Depression, however, is a clinical diagnosis with many more symptoms (such as overall hopelessness, despair, and loss of pleasure in life) than an unhappy mood. Psychoanalysts have traditionally described depression as primarily due to anger directed against the self (R. W. Firestone & Catlett 2009b).

- The critical inner voice says, *Sadness will last forever.* When we feel sad, it can seem as if sadness will never end. But this is not the case. We have to be patient and tolerant because being sad is something that we need to go through. It can't be rushed or avoided. When we are willing to stay with it and let it take its course, we come out better on the other end.

In his book, *Lincoln's Melancholy, How Depression Challenged a President and Fueled His Greatness*, Joshua Wolf Shenk quotes from Abraham Lincoln's letter consoling a friend (2006, 188–89):

In this sad world of ours, sorrow comes to all; and … it comes with bitterest agony…. Perfect relief is not possible, except with time. You cannot now believe that you will ever feel better…. And yet it is a mistake. You are sure to be happy again. Knowing this, which is certainly true, will make you some less miserable now. I have had enough experience to know what I say.

Oliver, too, had a critical inner voice coaching him not to feel sadness:

Oliver's critical inner voice said, *Those sad feelings you had the other night are bad news! Stay away from them. You saw what happened to your mother. She's been sad and depressed and miserable her whole life. Don't go near that emotion—it will ruin you forever.* He recognized that the voice came from his mother's views about life, and this insight made it easier for him to stand up for himself and confront the voice: "You don't know what you're talking about! It actually felt good to be sad about Dom. I was sad to feel trusting of someone after growing up so distrustful. And it's important to face sadness. I've felt it in therapy, and I got through the feeling and felt stronger for it." Oliver was determined to be alert to the critical inner voice that encouraged him to overwork and to cut himself off from feeling sad.

Journal Exercise 8.5. The Critical Inner Voice That Supports Misconceptions About Sadness

Think of what you believe about sadness, and consider that what you believe may be wrong. Then follow the first four adapted steps of the Voice Therapy method.

1. *Identify* your negative thoughts about sadness, using "I" statements to describe what sadness is and what it means. Write these statements down in your journal.

2. *Rewrite* your "I" statements as "you" statements in the form of warnings, orders, misinformation, or advice about sadness coming from your critical inner voice. Expand on them, continuing to rewrite them as "you" statements.

3. *Reflect* on what you have written, and record any new thoughts and insights.

4. *Confront* the warnings, orders, misinformation, or advice coming from your critical inner voice, using "I" statements to stand up for yourself and refute its misconceptions.

How to Face Sadness

It is vital to our well-being that we be able to accept our sadness and feel comfortable with it. When we defend against it and try to elude it, we interfere with our natural ability to process this emotion. Like any other avoidant response, steering clear of sad feelings not only increases our anxiety and tension but also exacerbates the intensity of our sadness.

When we try to numb ourselves to sadness, we invariably numb ourselves to all of our experiences. In the process of cutting off this one feeling, we necessarily end up blocking all our other feelings. The downside isn't just that we cut off the emotions that enhance our life, such as joy and excitement; it's also that we cut off the emotions that play a necessary role in our survival and self-preservation, such as fear and alarm. The more removed we are from our feelings, the more disengaged we become from ourselves and the more estranged we become from others, and the less capable we are to cope with life.

There are actions you can take that will better allow you to experience your sadness. One is to stop the defenses that are preventing you from feeling sadness. Another is to challenge the critical inner voice that is discouraging sadness. But the most significant action you can take is to remain open to feeling sadness.

Challenging Your Defenses Against Sadness

Quite simply, until you stop the defensive behavior that is cutting you off from feeling your emotions, you will not be able to feel sad. This is the most obvious step you can take to get in touch with your sad feelings, but it can also be the most difficult step because it usually involves confronting your addictive behavior. This kind of behavior can include all the obvious addictions (to drugs, alcohol, cigarettes, and other substances) as well as the more subtle addictions that can develop out of everyday activities when they are pursued compulsively, as discussed earlier in this chapter. Either way, you have to stop your defensive behavior before you can feel sadness.

As for addictions, learning to be tolerant of sad feelings actually helps in overcoming them, because avoidance of sadness is a driving force in addictive behavior. The Voice Therapy method is helpful in grappling with addiction because the critical inner voice is integral to the addictive process. You can learn to identify the critical inner voice that is encouraging your addiction, and you can then become aware of how it also punishes you for using. You can also be mindful of the critical inner voice that urges you to reengage in your addictive behavior after the fix has worn off. When you confront this voice and take action against it, you will feel strong and in control. You will no longer be the victim of your addiction.

Overcoming an addiction is always challenging, with many starts and stops and ups and downs. For this reason, it is vital to have a compassionate attitude toward yourself throughout the recovery process. Once you've realized that you have engaged in self-destructive behavior, you understand that allowing your critical inner voice to rip into you about it is never a constructive choice. You can acknowledge your misstep while maintaining a benevolent and realistic view of yourself as a developing human being who will make mistakes along the way. Recall Oliver, who adopted these attitudes as he took action against his addictive behavior and the critical inner voice that promoted it:

> After Oliver identified his critical inner voice and stood up for himself by confronting it, he thought of what he could do to control his tendency to lose himself in his work. The most

obvious possibility was to structure his time so that he couldn't slip into overworking. He looked at the tasks he actually needed to perform, and then he allotted reasonable amounts of time to accomplish them. He decided that he would not impulsively launch new projects but instead would thoroughly evaluate them and schedule them carefully. He also decided that he wouldn't work nights or weekends—and, equally important, Oliver decided to schedule time to be with Dom. While planning his week, Oliver set aside specific times for particular activities to share with Dom. He also allowed for periods of unplanned time together and spontaneous fun.

> ## Journal Exercise 8.6. Taking Action Against the Critical Inner Voice That Promotes Addictive Behavior
>
> Using your responses to journal exercise 8.2, think about the addictive behavior you uncovered, and about the critical inner voice that supports this behavior. Also think about what you said when you stood up for yourself and confronted your critical inner voice. Then, with these thoughts in mind, follow step 5 of Voice Therapy and *plan* the actions you will take to counter the critical inner voice that promotes addictive behavior. Write these actions down, being detailed and specific about what you will do with respect to particular people, communication, behavior, situations, and so on. You will *implement* your plan in step 6 of Voice Therapy.

Challenge Your Critical Inner Voice

Be on the alert for when the critical inner voice feeds you misinformation about sadness, and then actively disregard the voice. For example, instead of believing that sadness is an abnormal emotion, treat sadness as what it is—a natural part of life. You can reject the idea that sadness is bad for you by taking advantage of any opportunity to feel sad. Stop reacting to sadness as if it were depression! Don't be afraid of it—it is not overwhelming or everlasting. Adopting the attitude that sadness is normal and healthy will counter your critical inner voice and make you more comfortable with this intrinsic human emotion.

Journal Exercise 8.7. Taking Action Against the Critical Inner Voice That Supports Misconceptions About Sadness

Using your responses to journal exercise 8.5, think about the misconceptions you uncovered regarding sadness, and about the critical inner voice that supports these misconceptions. Also think about what you said when you confronted your critical inner voice and its misconceptions. Then, with these thoughts in mind, follow step 5 of Voice Therapy and *plan* the actions you will take to counter the critical inner voice that supports misconceptions about sadness. Write these actions down, being detailed and specific about what you will do with respect to particular people, communication, behavior, situations, and so on. You will *implement* your plan in step 6 of Voice Therapy.

Allow Sadness in Yourself and Others

By the time we reach adulthood, we are largely programmed to avoid sadness. Typically, we feel shame when we are sad. We are embarrassed if we tear up, and we are often uncomfortable in the presence of someone who is crying—we have learned to look away, almost instinctively.

Most of us grew up learning not to cry. Most parents make a point of never crying in front of their children. Babies are shushed or quickly soothed when they begin to sob. Children are ridiculed the minute their bottom lip starts to quiver. We come to regard sadness as a negative emotion, a stigma that should be hidden if it can't be avoided. We learn this lesson in our families, and society reinforces it. The widow who doesn't weep at her husband's funeral may be praised for being strong; the child who fights back his tears is a "big boy."

Avoiding sadness is especially detrimental to a relationship. Sidestepping sadness when it comes up kills the closeness and magic of an intimate moment. And if we repress sadness, it becomes more difficult for us to achieve deeper intimacy with others, including our partner. For this reason, it is important to actively encourage sadness. Resist the temptation to avoid sad feelings when they are aroused in you, or in your partner. Don't make a joke or change the subject. Don't make a comment to lighten the mood. Don't even look away. Remain engaged and present so that the sadness can be a shared experience. When we share our most sensitive and vulnerable emotions, we are at our most open and undefended with each other.

Journal Exercise 8.8. Taking Action to Allow for Sadness

Using your responses to the journal exercises in this chapter, think about the different ways you have of cutting off sadness, and about the critical inner voice that supports this behavior. Then, with these thoughts in mind, follow step 5 of Voice Therapy and *plan* the actions you will take to allow for sadness. Write these actions down, being detailed and specific about what you will do with respect to particular people, communication, behavior, situations, and so on. You will *implement* your plan in step 6 of Voice Therapy.

Summary and a Look Ahead

The tender feelings we experience in an intimate relationship often arouse a poignant sense of sadness in ourselves as well as in our partner. Sadness is something that most of us go to great lengths to avoid, using all kinds of defensive maneuvers. But we need to tolerate and value sadness as a natural consequence of genuine affection and love, and as a life-affirming emotion. When we stop defending ourselves from sadness, we are more open to all our emotions. We are less cynical and more tolerant. We develop compassion for ourselves, which we can then feel toward others. We become more likely to thrive—and to have love in our lives. In the words of the poet and writer Kahlil Gibran (1996, 16), "The deeper that sorrow carves into your being, the more joy you can contain." If we have no tolerance for the sadness that love can arouse, we have no capacity for the joy we can feel in loving, and we have nothing to counteract the fear of loss that is also a consequence of love, as we'll see in the following chapter.

CHAPTER 9

When Love Stirs Up
Our Fear of Loss

Death is our friend precisely because it brings us into absolute and passionate presence with all that is here, that is natural, that is love.

—Rainer Maria Rilke, letter to Countess Margot Sizzo-Noris-Crouy

By the time we reach adulthood and try to establish an intimate relationship, we are fairly well defended and guarded. We have habits that diminish how much we feel, and attitudes that restrict how open and vulnerable we are. We have a critical inner voice that attacks us, berates others, and warns us about the dangers of love. But even as we overcome these barriers and form a close relationship with someone, all is not sunshine and roses. This is because love arouses our fear of loss, including our angst about death. As we come to dearly love and cherish another person, the fact that we will eventually lose him or her causes us anxiety. At the same time, love heightens the feeling of valuing our own lives and ourselves, and this in turn increases our fear of our own death.

Love, the very feeling that makes life so worth living, also brings to our awareness the reality that our precious existence is both fragile and temporary. It makes us conscious of endings and frightened of losing what we have. Great works of art, such as the tragedies of Shakespeare, the operas of Puccini and Verdi, and the poetry of Yeats, express both the agony and the ecstasy of this paradoxical situation. The hard truth is that there is no fairy-tale ending; there is no "ever after" that two people can live happily. Every relationship ends tragically, because of either natural causes (one of the partners dies) or unnatural causes (the love between them does not survive).

This chapter offers information to help you live and love while fully acknowledging the reality and impact of death. The chapter will help you realize that fear of loss and death anxiety are activated by negative as well as positive events, love being the most positive trigger, and therefore one of the strongest. It will also help you understand the defensive reactions you use to cut off death awareness. The chapter's journal exercises will help you become more aware of your fear of loss and your death anxiety. You'll learn how to recognize the way your critical inner voice intensifies and supports these feelings, and to plan actions that you can take to counter these fears. Overall, the chapter will help you see that you can deal with your anxiety about death and live with existential questions that have no answers or solutions.

How Death Anxiety Is Aroused

Robert defines death anxiety as both unconscious anxiety about and conscious realization of the fact that our lives are terminal and that we face separation from loved ones (R. W. Firestone 1994; R. W. Firestone & Catlett 2009a). However, most people are rarely aware of experiencing death anxiety, and many have no idea what this concept means.

To get a better idea of what death anxiety is, think about how a child feels when she first becomes aware that all living beings die. You may remember your own experience of learning this truth when you were young. Or in your adult life, you may have witnessed a child grappling with this agonizing discovery. But even if you have no memory or direct experience, you can imagine and empathize with the trauma of a child who is confronted with the reality that everything she holds dear will come to an end. As we saw in chapter 1, when we were children, we cut ourselves off from our conscious awareness of death and drove it into our subconscious. We then lived with the subliminal fear that this horror would resurface.

As adults, anything that reminds us of death threatens to unlock the terror that we suppressed in childhood. Both negative and positive events can trigger our awareness of death and thus our death anxiety. We react by defending ourselves and listening to the critical inner voice, which alarms us about death and loss. In truth, however, the unbearable death anxiety that we anticipate experiencing is actually the intense response we had as children. But this primal reaction is very different from what we feel as adults when we face the issue of death.

Negative Triggers

In our daily lives, we are repeatedly assaulted by reminders of mortality. The news media report tragedies. Acquaintances are diagnosed with serious diseases. TV shows feature graphic depictions of violence. And little children ask questions about what happens when you die. We are given advice for our own good—buckle up, get a flu shot, don't eat "bad" fat, don't walk in certain neighborhoods. The implication is clear: *If you don't heed these warnings, you will die.*

The most obvious way in which death awareness is brought to our consciousness is through direct reminders and actual events. These can be as hard-hitting as driving past a fatal car accident or learning that a friend has died. Or they can be subtle, such as hearing someone comment, "I just haven't felt the same since my uncle's funeral" or "My mother is going for another scan, and I'm so worried her cancer has come back." Consider the example of Jack, who was not conscious that his death anxiety had been aroused by the death of his fiancée's father:

> Jack had been living with Sonia for two years when her father died. Sonia felt a mixture of emotions—she was heartbroken because she and her father had been close, but she was also angry at her father for having neglected his health. Most of all, though, she missed him.

Jack felt for Sonia's loss and admired how she was handling her pain. She shared her sorrow with him, but she didn't drag him down or pull on him to lift her spirits. She sought grief counseling for help with what she was going through.

Jack had only met Sonia's father a few times, so even though he felt sympathy for her, the death wasn't a personal loss for him. But over the next several weeks, Jack began to pull away from Sonia. He hung out more with friends after work and came home later than usual. He began playing golf most weekends. When he was home, he watched TV and then went to bed without saying much.

Jack began to feel lonely and realized he had been avoiding Sonia. He began to wonder why he'd been distancing himself from her. It wasn't her—she was being open and loving. It wasn't her father's death—he hadn't really known the man. He wondered if it was something more personal to him.

His thoughts went to his own father, who was much older than Sonia's had been. Jack felt sad as he pictured how devastated he would be if his father died. He realized that the death of Sonia's father had awakened his anxiety about losing his own father.

Positive Triggers

One reason why it can be difficult to pinpoint what has triggered our fear of loss and our death anxiety is that we often look for the trigger in the wrong place. And of course it makes sense to look to some negative event for the cause of an adverse emotional reaction. But the source often turns out instead to be some positive occurrence. This concept is counterintuitive, however, so we may overlook this explanation and then fail to recognize why our fear of loss or our death anxiety has been stirred up. Whatever the positive event may have been, it has made us value ourselves and our lives and left us with the feeling that we have more to lose. The most meaningful positive events that we react to in this way involve the experience of closeness and intimacy in a loving relationship. For this reason, love can bring up death anxiety and strong fear of loss.

The fear of separation and loss that is often induced by love can be attributed to several different aspects of intimacy (R. W. Firestone & Catlett 1999). As we fall in love, develop a more serious attachment to our partner, and commit ourselves to him or her, it is natural for us to fear the loss of the person in whom we are becoming so invested. This fear can reawaken primitive feelings related to early experiences of separation and abandonment.

Love can also intensify our awareness of our own death. When someone we love simply loves us for who we are, our sense of self is strengthened. In seeing ourselves through the eyes of someone who loves and values us, we come to appreciate who we are, and to value our own existence. In addition, feeling particularly loving toward another person brings us into contact with a part of ourselves that is often unfamiliar to us. To feel interest, caring, compassion, tenderness, empathy, and selflessness is to find our experience of life enhanced. This is what people mean when they say, "Love has made me the best version of myself."

But being the best version of ourselves is frightening. According to Abraham Maslow (1971, 34), "We fear our highest possibilities.... We are generally afraid to become that which we can glimpse in our most perfect moments." In "our most perfect moments," we have the most to lose—life is at its most precious, and the reality of its ultimate end is all the more agonizing. Monica, for example, experienced heightened death anxiety after feeling especially loving toward her husband:

> Monica and Steve went through a tough time in their marriage, and they had been close to divorcing. But couples therapy helped them deal with the issues that were causing their problems, and a year later they felt that their relationship was back on track.
>
> Then Steve suggested that the two of them go to Hawaii for a week. Monica was delighted. They thoroughly enjoyed their vacation, taking pleasure in romance as well as in each other's company. But a few nights before they were scheduled

to return home, Monica started to worry about the flight. She had obsessive thoughts that their plane would crash, and this preoccupation was distracting her from the good time she was having with Steve.

Monica confided in him, but no amount of reasoning or logic could relieve her worries. Steve sensed that the problem didn't have to do with fear of flying but rather with some deeper fear. He encouraged Monica to talk about her feelings, and she described how, on this trip, she had felt herself developing an even stronger commitment to him. As she expressed the depth of her feeling, she also felt how afraid she was of losing him.

Monica felt relief after talking with Steve, and the next day she noticed that her obsessive thoughts had diminished. Their conversation opened them up more to each other and left both of them feeling even closer than during the first part of their trip.

Journal Exercise 9.1. Your Reactions to Anxiety About Loss and Death

Read through the following scenarios, which represent situations in which death anxiety is often aroused. If you've experienced any of these situations, write about what you felt at the time.

- Someone close to me passed away.

- A person I admired died unexpectedly.

- I was watching a movie in which the hero died.

- I passed by a terrible traffic accident.

- I was consoling a child about death.

- I was imagining a loved one's death.

- I heard that someone I knew had a life-threatening illness.

- My pet died.

- I read a book in which a beloved character died.

- I saw an old friend and was reminded of time passing.

- My partner and I had a very personal conversation.

- I realized how much my partner means to me.

- My partner and I had a particularly close and passionate sexual experience.

- My partner was especially loving toward me.

- My partner and I talked about moving in together (getting married, having a baby, etc.).

Can you think of any other events or occasions that aroused your awareness of death? Write about them in your journal.

Now think about how you react to your awareness of mortality. Read through the following examples, and write about any of these reactions you may have had.

- I became unusually withdrawn and quiet.

- I felt less enthusiastic in general.

- I seemed to be less invested in my life.

- I distanced myself from my partner.

- I picked a fight with my partner.

- I drank more or too much.

- I smoked a lot of cigarettes.

- I overate or binged.

- I stuffed myself with sweets or junk food.

Can you think of any other reactions you've had when your awareness of death was aroused? Write about them in your journal.

How the Critical Inner Voice Intensifies Death Anxiety and Fear of Loss

When death anxiety is aroused, whether by negative or positive causes, it produces the critical inner voice that warns us not to invest in life, and especially not to develop a meaningful relationship. Sometimes this voice deals directly with death and existential issues: *It's too painful when people die! Don't care about anyone* or *So what if you're in love now? It won't last—nothing lasts forever.* What's different about this type of attack by the critical inner voice is that it's not based on distortions or long-held misperceptions. It's based on reality—we *are* going to die. So how do you deal with this particular type of attack by your critical inner voice?

When you confront an attack that warns you about death, it is important to focus on the *intent* of the message rather than on its *content.* What your critical inner voice is saying may be true, but the voice's motives are malicious and must be challenged. Your critical inner voice is using a truth about life to turn you against yourself. For example, the voice is right about the fact that nothing lasts forever. But that's not the salient point. The issue is that your critical inner voice is taking advantage of an existential reality in order to manipulate you into divesting from love. You cannot confront this type of attack by addressing the facts. You can't deny the truth ("You're wrong—I'm not going to die"), but you also can't agree with your critical inner voice ("You're right—I'm going to die, so I should give up"). You have to confront the voice's intent: "You are using this point to get me to give up on myself and my life. Yes, I am going to die. But I am alive now, and I won't let you frighten me into not living my life to the fullest!" Jack stood up to precisely this kind of attack from his critical inner voice:

> Jack realized that his critical inner voice was telling him, *When your father dies, you're going to feel horrible. You can't even stand thinking about it. You can't even tolerate Sonia's grief about her father!*

He felt passionate when he confronted his critical inner voice: "I am going to feel very sad when my father dies. I love him, and he's important to me. It will be a huge loss. But I'm not going to back away from those feelings. I can tolerate them. And I'm not going to keep backing away from Sonia to avoid those feelings."

Jack talked with Sonia about what he had been thinking, and he apologized to her for having been distant. Afterward, he found it easier to be emotionally available to her.

At other times when our death anxiety is aroused, the critical inner voice doesn't address death directly. Instead, it warns us against investing in life and love. It persuades us to withdraw from the people who matter to us, and from activities that are personally meaningful: *You're better off keeping to yourself* or *Maybe he isn't right for you—you should end the relationship.* In this case, the critical inner voice influences us to withdraw from life and, in effect, erase the contrast between fully living and dying by aligning ourselves with death. This type of attack by the critical inner voice also needs to be confronted directly: "I'm not listening to you. I like being with my friends. I don't like being alone all the time" or "I'm not paying attention to your negative way of looking at my life. I love him. Leave me alone." Address the critical inner voice that tries to manipulate you into backing away from vital parts of your life: "You're trying to get me to give up everything that's important to me. Do you think this will protect me from hurt or loss or tragedy? You're wrong." When we make an effort to be conscious of attacks like these by our critical inner voice, we are freer to give full rein to our happiness and our loving feelings.

Death Anxiety and Fear of Loss at Different Stages of a Relationship

Death anxiety and fear related to loss can be aroused at various stages of a relationship, and when they are, the critical inner voice heightens them in a manner that interferes with the ability to achieve and maintain intimacy. Some people are so highly reactive that their fear can be triggered by the mere anticipation of being close to another person. Their critical inner voice prevents them from even initiating a relationship: *Do you really want to get involved? You're better off on your own and unattached* or *Someday you'll want a relationship, but not now. Wait until you're ready.* Other people enter into a relationship and enjoy the beginning phase. But when their feelings become stronger and they invest more emotionally, they become apprehensive about future losses, and their critical inner voice may say, *This is getting too serious. If she stops loving you, you'll be devastated* or *Are you sure you want to commit to this type of involvement? If things fall apart, you'll lose everything.*

People who by nature are less reactive to death awareness and potential loss are better able to establish a loving and meaningful relationship. Somewhere along the way, however, they too may reach a point where their fear is aroused. This often happens when some event—buying a house, for example, or getting married, or beginning a family—takes on the significance of a shared future. Such an event implies, "Until death do us part" and triggers the critical inner voice to say things like *Is this what you really want to do? This means forever— until the end!* or *You're talking about a lifetime. You're talking about getting old. You're talking about all the rest of your years!*

It's important to confront the critical inner voice that tries to sabotage love for the purpose of relieving anxiety about loss or death. For example, to confront the voice that keeps you from entering a relationship, you can say, "I know I'm anxious, but I want to have a relationship. I don't want to keep avoiding it." To confront the voice that interferes with your relationship's becoming more intimate, you can say, "I know I will have more to lose if I allow this relationship to get more serious, but it will be worth it. I don't want to protect myself just so I won't be scared." To confront the voice that warns you against lifelong commitments, you can say, "Yes, this means forever. That's how much this relationship means to me. I'm in this to the end, even though it frightens me." Let's return now to the example of Monica:

When Monica began to feel more deeply committed to Steve, the critical inner voice played to her fear of loss: *Don't make this kind of investment! Don't let anyone mean this much to you. Otherwise, you'll be emotionally shattered when he dies. Don't be a fool!*

Monica angrily confronted her critical inner voice: "Being seriously committed feels good. I *like* standing by what's important to me! I don't want to minimize my love or my feelings to protect myself from how I might feel in the future."

Journal Exercise 9.2. The Critical Inner Voice That Intensifies Fear of Loss and Anxiety About Death

Using your responses to journal exercise 9.1, think about your experiences of loss and death. Then follow the first four adapted steps of the Voice Therapy method.

1. *Identify* a particular type of fearful thought you have, using "I" statements to describe how this thought predicts loss and warns you to be self-protective. Write these statements down in your journal.

2. *Rewrite* your "I" statements as "you" statements in the form of attacks coming from your critical inner voice. Expand on them, continuing to rewrite them as "you" statements.

3. *Reflect* on what you have written, and record any new thoughts and insights.

4. *Confront* the attacks coming from your critical inner voice, using "I" statements to stand up for yourself.

Defensive Reactions to Death Awareness and Fear of Loss

Awareness of death and fear of loss make us conscious that we are ultimately not in control of our lives. This knowledge hits us hardest where we feel most defenseless and out of control—in our love relationship. We typically react by defending ourselves, in an effort to get our lives seemingly back under control. To do so, we employ the same defenses discussed throughout this book. We stop being vulnerable, to protect ourselves from loss. We cling to a fantasy bond so as not to feel alone. We return to an old, negative identity or re-create our past so we can feel safe. Or we engage in self-destructive behavior to cut ourselves off from our feelings.

Another defensive reaction to death anxiety and fear of loss is to preserve the illusion of being better than other people. Vanity and a narcissistic orientation can imbue us with the conviction that we are special or above others. We may also maintain what we regard as an elevated position by attaching ourselves to a group or belief system that we consider superior to all others. On an unconscious level, this delusion of being above mere mortals supports a fantasy of immortality. This defense is easily threatened by any reminder that we are just like other people—that we are, in fact, mortal.

Whenever we engage in any of these defenses against death anxiety or fear of loss, we retreat from life. Our self-protective stance cuts us off from our feeling for ourselves and also diminishes our need for affiliation with anyone else. Taking this position has a devastating effect on an intimate relationship. To give up our wants and priorities as a reaction to these fears is to lessen our overall investment in life. A twisted but simplistic logic persuades us that we can elude death by eliminating life.

How the Critical Inner Voice Supports Defensive Reactions to Death Anxiety and Fear of Loss

The critical inner voice doesn't just heighten our anxiety about death. It also encourages us to defend ourselves against our awareness of death. It prevails upon us to be invulnerable, establish a fantasy bond, maintain our old identity, re-create our past, and engage in self-destructive behavior.

The critical inner voice that supports vanity and narcissism builds you up: *You're such an amazing person! Your partner is so lucky to be with you* or *You're the one who really knows what's going on in this relationship.* At the same time, it tears your partner down: *He just isn't as smart as you are* or *She doesn't have your capacity for love.* Because the critical inner voice sounds complimentary, you may find it hard to identify this voice as harmful. But the fact that it is trying to separate you from other people is an indication that it is destructive. You can confront this critical inner voice by saying, "I don't like being special and superior—it's lonely, and it's a lie" or "I'm not smarter than he is" or "We're both equally capable of loving, and equally worthy of love" and finally "I'm just a person like everyone else, and that's good enough."

There is also the critical inner voice that appeals to your vanity by warning you that you are being disrespected or disregarded: *Your partner should be paying more attention to you* or *He isn't doing what you say* or *She isn't listening to you.* Again, this voice may seem to have your interests in mind, but taking its warnings seriously will make you distrustful of your partner. To confront this voice, you can say, "I don't like your victimized views of me and your paranoia about my partner—no one is against me" or "I'm not being disrespected or ignored. If my partner isn't constantly attending to me, that doesn't mean he doesn't care about me."

Keep in mind that the critical inner voice is clever and devious. It uses our intelligence against us in order to rationalize pushing away love. Our reasons for defending ourselves from intimacy may seem logical, but they're aimed at dulling or obscuring our underlying fear of death and dying.

Journal Exercise 9.3. Taking Action Against the Critical Inner Voice That Intensifies Death Anxiety and Fear of Loss

Using your responses to journal exercise 9.2, consider the particular type of fearful thought you have that predicts loss and warns you to be self-protective, and consider the critical inner voice that supports this thought. Also consider what you said when you stood up for yourself and confronted your critical inner voice. Then, with these thoughts in mind, follow step 5 of Voice Therapy and *plan* the actions you will take to counter the critical inner voice that intensifies fear of loss and anxiety about death. Write these actions down, being detailed and specific about what you will do with respect to particular people, communication, behavior, situations, and so on. You will *implement* your plan in step 6 of Voice Therapy.

How to Live with Death Awareness

Our fear of loss and our anxiety about death are not irrational or unfounded. They are natural reactions to an existential issue that is real and has no resolution. We were filled with horror during childhood when we first became aware of death, and now we unconsciously expect to be overwhelmed again at any moment by the same primal feeling in all its original intensity. Our dread of experiencing the same terror we felt back then keeps us stuck in an unconscious state of fearful anticipation and mounting tension. And it keeps us from facing the issue today, as adults who can live with the reality of death and future loss.

So how do we live with death awareness? The answer seems to lie in two virtually universal responses that many people have when the critical inner voice arouses their death anxiety and fear of loss. One response is "Don't tell me I can't stand to face the reality of death. I can stand it. It's a fact of life. Sure, it scares me. The unknown scares me. But I can face it." And the other is "Yes, my life is going to end. But that's all the more reason for me to value it and make the most of the life I have. I don't want to give up my life to make dying easier. I want to appreciate it even more and invest in it 100 percent!"

The truth is that you can tolerate your sadness about the finality of a loved one's life, and about the finality of your own life as well. When you are made aware of death, you can let yourself experience your agonizing emotions and fully feel your pain and sadness. And as you release these feelings, they will subside. You will feel relieved and more in touch with your real self.

The Positive Effect of Death Awareness

Even though death awareness tends to cause us to react negatively, it also has the potential to have a powerfully positive impact on our life. The fact that life is limited makes life all the more meaningful and precious. Its finality can inspire us to make the most of the time we have on Earth. We can use this awareness to our advantage, enlisting it to help us become more fully engaged with life, continue challenging and developing ourselves as unique individuals, and develop loving personal relationships. Even under the most challenging circumstances, as when we are facing death directly, we can be inspired to remain invested in life and to value love.

The story of our friend Fred Branfman illustrates this very fact. We met Fred in the late 1990s, after he'd seen Robert's documentary *Life, Death and Denial.* He was fifty-seven years old and lived in Budapest with his wife, Zsuzsa, with whom he had a passionate and sometimes tempestuous relationship. Fred visited us every year in California and stayed for at least a month.

Fred had been a political activist and author (Branfman 1972) as well as a political consultant. Then, one night in 1986, after his father's death, Fred had awakened with an agonizing awareness of his own death, an awareness that was ultimately transformed into a deep love for life. He left the political arena and dedicated himself to developing his concept of life-affirming death awareness. Fred often said that his most excruciating experiences of death awareness were when he pictured his life without Zsuzsa, or hers without him.

One year when Fred came to visit, he complained of not feeling well. He was seventy-two years old at the time. Medical tests revealed that he was suffering from amyotrophic lateral sclerosis (ALS, also known as Lou Gehrig's disease). He debated what to do in relation to Zsuzsa. Should he go home? Should he stay in California and spare her the agony of what he was going to have to face? He realized that his critical inner voice was advising him: *Don't go back to Budapest— Zsuzsa won't be able to take it. She's an emotionally fragile person, and she is going to fall apart. Stay here, and spare her the ordeal.* Fred confronted the voice: "Stop predicting how she's going to react! It's impossible to know. I don't want to protect myself, or her. I don't want to underestimate her, either. I love her and want to be close to her, especially now. If she can't tolerate it, then I can come back to California. But I have to take the chance." Afterward, Fred was no longer confused about what to do—he wanted to fly home to Budapest, and Zsuzsa.

Shortly after he got home, I received an email from Fred with the following paragraph:

> It feels like almost a miracle, but the best thing by far has been that I am having the "transformed" connection with Zsuzsa that I have always dreamed of. From my perspective, she has been incredibly loving, upbeat, supportive emotionally and practically, wise, understanding, kind, empathetic when I am down but doing her best to bring me up—I could go on. Any problems we've had in the past seem to have disappeared. Every moment we spend together feels precious to me. I find myself really appreciating various moments in my life in ways I have not before.

Five months later, on September 24, we received an email from Zsuzsa telling us that Fred had died (see *The Economist* 2014). Robert and I were deeply pained by this news. But we were also glad that Fred hadn't acted on the critical inner voice that had advised him not to go home and be with Zsuzsa. During their last months together, their awareness of Fred's impending death had enabled them to appreciate and fully feel the love they had for and from each other. Zsuzsa included this message in her email:

> When we said goodbye to each other, we both felt comforted by a profound feeling of contentment that our life together has come full circle, our love for each other complete, that over the years, we learned to love and to be loved for the very first time in our lives. We would dearly have loved to share more of the same, yet we both know there was nothing more that we wanted that we didn't already have.

The experience of Fred and Zsuzsa exemplifies how realizing the temporary nature of life in an undefended state of mind can heighten our awareness of how precious each moment is and increase the likelihood that we will invest more of ourselves in our relationships.

Summary and a Look Ahead

At our most loving and affectionate, our most open and vulnerable, when we are especially valuing our own life and our loved one's existence, we can become agonizingly aware of how much we have to lose. It takes courage to be close to another person in a romantic relationship with the awareness that, inevitably, it will end. But our awareness of future loss can also enhance our life and our love relationship. Our awareness of death can put life in perspective and make us cognizant of what really matters. As the poet Emily Dickinson wrote, "That it will never come again / Is what makes life so sweet" (Dickinson 1955). In this sense, love not only instigates death awareness but also shows us life's ultimate value. The final chapter of this book will help you realize that value as you learn how to preserve your individuality, develop your communication skills, and deal constructively with anger so that you can be fully engaged in the act of loving.

CHAPTER 10

A Look Ahead

Falling in love was simple; one had only to yield. Digesting another person, however, and sustaining love, was bloody work, and not a soft job.

> —Hanif Kureishi, "Girl," in *Midnight All Day: Stories*

What happens once you stop pushing love away? When you remove the psychological barriers that are interfering with love, what do you have? What's it like when you dare to love?

Once we challenge the various ways in which we are defending ourselves against love, our relationship has a chance to thrive. We are able to accept genuine affection and love. Because we are more vulnerable, our interactions typically involve an ongoing exchange of kindnesses, generosity, and affection. Because we are rejecting our negative identity, we are better able to tolerate someone seeing us as unique and desirable, an awareness that connects us to positive feelings of personal worth.

Since we have committed ourselves to challenging the elements of a fantasy bond in our relationship, our time with our partner is based on free choice rather than obligation. We choose our partner on the basis of love, not need. In fact, ongoing choice rather than habit helps us maintain our original excitement. We have a basic unwillingness to allow our relationship to become deadened, dull, or routine. We're devoted to keeping our romantic spark alive rather than preserving a habitual style of relating.

We now realize that loving and being loved, as well as valuing ourselves and our experience, can lead to feelings of sadness and fear of loss. Because we regard sadness as part of a healthy relationship, we share tender, poignant exchanges with our partner.

Perhaps most significant, we place high value on continuing to build a good relationship. We now know that loving is a skill and that, like any other skill, it can be developed with knowledge and effort. This chapter suggests actions that will help you continue to counter the critical inner voice that is trying to impair love. The chapter also explains how you can continue using the Voice Therapy method when problems inevitably come up in your relationship. It offers advice for developing personal qualities that will benefit you as an individual in your relationship, and it encourages you to treat your partner in ways that are respectful and supportive. In addition, it shows you how to communicate as well as how to handle your angry feelings. Finally, the chapter breaks down the steps of the act of loving. The chapter's journal exercises will help you reflect on these suggestions and advice and apply them to your life.

Continuing to Use the Voice Therapy Method

Now that you understand why you sabotage love, and now that you have mastered the tools for challenging that behavior, you undoubtedly feel more empowered. But issues invariably arise between two people sharing their lives. When an issue arises between you and your partner, you can identify the critical inner voice that is contributing to the problem, and then you can plan and implement action against that voice.

Change is not quick or easy, especially when you are trying to alter defensive patterns you have depended on for most of your life. It will take time and hard work, and compassion for yourself, to adjust your way of being in your relationship. When you run into trouble, you can get back on track with your partner and yourself by using journaling and applying the adapted steps of the Voice Therapy method:

1. *Identify* the behavior, attitude, or emotion that is causing you trouble today, using "I" statements to express any thoughts you're having that promote or justify this behavior, attitude, or emotion, and to describe what you're doing, thinking, or feeling.

2. *Rewrite* your "I" statements as "you" statements in the form of attacks coming from your critical inner voice. Expand on them, continuing to rewrite them as "you" statements.

3. *Reflect* on what you have written, and record any new thoughts and insights.

4. *Confront* the attacks coming from your critical inner voice, using "I" statements to stand up for yourself.

5. *Plan* the actions you will take to counter the critical inner voice that supports this behavior, attitude, or emotion. Write these actions down, being detailed and specific about what you will do with respect to particular people, communication, behavior, situations, and so on. (You will *implement* your plan in step 6 of Voice Therapy.)

After you have used this method for a while, you will begin to see patterns in the attacks coming from your critical inner voice. You will realize that specific events tend to trigger it, and that certain themes recur. In a sense, you will come to know your enemy within and become good at spotting it. You will also become more familiar with the actions you can take to go against this inner enemy. Recall Calvin, whom we met in chapter 6; he continued to use the Voice Therapy method to deal with his critical inner voice when it told him he was an unattractive nerd:

> While Calvin was dating Elena, there were times when his critical inner voice was especially strong. When he and Elena became romantically and sexually involved, Calvin had the

thought that she couldn't possibly be attracted to him. He rephrased that thought as an attack coming from his critical inner voice, and he was able counter the voice and not let it influence his behavior.

Calvin and Elena were together for six months. When Elena ended the relationship, Calvin had self-hating thoughts. Once again, he converted these thoughts into attacks coming from his critical inner voice. Then he stood up to the voice, an action that helped him take his own side. Overall, he felt more self-assured as a result of having challenged his critical inner voice during his six months with Elena.

A few months after his relationship with Elena ended, Calvin met Sarah at a party. He felt comfortable flirting with her and expressing his interest in her. They developed a serious relationship, and Calvin continued to confront his critical inner voice whenever it tried to undermine his self-confidence.

Preserving Individuality to Strengthen Your Relationship

Two fundamental factors contributing to the success of your relationship are your own continued development as an individual and your appreciation and support for your partner's individuality. To this end, you are learning to value your independence and striving to maintain your integrity by remaining adult, open, undefended, and honest in your interactions. You are also learning to respect the fact that your partner is a sovereign individual, separate from you and your relationship. A relationship thrives when two strong individuals bring their distinctive and varied qualities to their partnership.

Maintaining Your Individuality

To be a better person in your life and a good partner in your relationship, it's critical that you strive to maintain a strong sense of independence and autonomy and a well-developed point of view. With this ongoing goal, you can continue to cultivate and strengthen your unique traits as well as behavior that reflects your interests and ideals. In your relationship, you need to be careful that you are not looking for someone to complete your incompleteness or to define or affirm you.

Be adult. It's common for people to complain of their partner being immature and refusing to grow up. Being adult is not just a question of emotionally mature behavior. Being truly adult also involves recognizing your early childhood trauma and losses, taking steps to resolve them, and understanding how they helped shape your current behavior. It means actively identifying and challenging the defenses you formed as a child and correcting the negative attitudes or biases you acquired.

Be open and undefended. Openness involves the ability to be forthright in revealing and expressing your personal feelings, thoughts, dreams, and desires. Being nondefensive and open to feedback is one of the most valuable relationship skills you can develop. Instead of defending yourself from your partner's criticisms or suggestions, you can look for the kernel of truth in what your partner is saying, because it may offer you an opportunity for personal growth. When you're concerned in this way with your development as an individual, you can remain open to change in your intimate relationship but also retain your sense of self, your strength, and your individuality.

Being honest is vital to your integrity as an individual, and necessary to the development of trust in your close relationship. It's best to be honest even when telling the truth is hard. When you are deceptive or directly untruthful with your partner, you betray yourself, and you fracture your partner's sense of reality. You also damage the trust and closeness between you. Love requires truth because without truth you can't build and maintain the trust that is essential to an intimate relationship.

Supporting Your Partner's Individuality

Respect your partner by encouraging your partner's unique interests and personal goals, independent of your own. Be sensitive to your partner's wants, desires, and feelings, and place as much value on them as you do on your own. This type of interest in and feeling for your partner is altruistic and goes beyond any selfish or self-serving concerns you may have.

In order to achieve this level of regard, you need to have empathy with and compassion for your partner. This involves using your mind as well as your emotions and intuition to perceive and vicariously experience the nature of your loved one. When you understand your partner in this deeply empathetic manner, you are aware of what you have in common, but you also recognize and value your differences. Maggie and Gretchen, whom we met in chapter 5, were determined to reestablish the equality in their relationship:

> Maggie dealt with her childishness and dependency by working hard to develop her sense of herself. She challenged herself to function as an independent adult. She communicated honestly and directly, and she was interested and nondefensive during interactions.
>
> Gretchen, for her part, learned to be respectful of Maggie as a person separate from and equal to her. As she came to know Maggie in this way, she was able to realize and appreciate Maggie's distinctive qualities.

Journal Exercise 10.1. Your Thoughts About Yourself and Your Partner as Individuals

Reflect on the following prompts, and record your thoughts in your journal.

- What are some of my personal interests that are different from my partner's? Am I actively pursuing them?

- Do I look to my partner for definition or direction? In what ways do I do this?

- Do I regard my partner as my missing piece?

- Do I look to my partner to compensate for any of my short-comings? If so, in what ways?

- Do I use my partner to relieve my insecurities or loneliness?

- Am I an adult in my life and in my relationship? Do I act childish or parental?

- Am I open and nondefensive in my interactions?

- Do I strive to be honest when I communicate?

- Do I have integrity in my life? Do my actions and my words communicate the same message?

- What are some of my partner's personal interests that are unique to him or her?

- Am I supportive of my partner's interests? Do I respect them as much as I respect my own?

- Am I threatened by my partner's separate interests?

- Do I act discouraging or belittling or dismissive of my partner's separate interests?

- How is my partner different from me? Which differences do I like? Which ones do I dislike?

- Am I successful in empathizing with my partner? Am I able to feel what my partner is experiencing as a person?

- Are there any gender stereotypes that are hurting the respect that my partner and I have for each other in our relationship?

Developing the Skills for Communicating in an Intimate Relationship

Communication is simply a matter of talking and listening, but it's a mistake to think that communicating is simple. Talking and listening are innate abilities, but the ability to communicate—to speak openly and hear what someone else is saying—is anything but. To have a successful relationship, you need to develop the skills of talking *with* and listening *to* another person. Without these skills, you and your partner will be handicapped in your intimate relationship.

People who know how to communicate always follow one rule when they enter into a conversation: *Give up the need to be right.* A conversation is not a battle that you have to win. You don't have anything to prove. You know that working things out between you can be a messy process, and you expect to have reactions. You may become angry and frustrated, or something your partner says may provoke you. But through it all, you respect the fact that your partner may have something to say that is worth listening to and thinking about.

Effective communicating with your partner involves three skills:

1. Talking with your partner

2. Listening to your partner

3. Reflecting on what you have learned from your conversation

Talking with Your Partner

In a conversation, there is only one thing you can be sure of—what you are thinking about or feeling in the moment. You can be sure of nothing else—not your partner's thoughts, feelings, or perceptions, and not even the reality of what is going on between the two of you. For this reason, the only subject you can talk about with any authority is yourself and how you are feeling.

Focus on what you can say about yourself in real time—not on what you can say about your partner or the kids or work or your friends, just on what you can say about yourself. Acknowledge your irrational feelings. Don't dismiss them as inappropriate, immature, or meaningless. Make an effort to talk about feelings that you would much rather skip over or hide, feelings that you fear will cause you embarrassment or humiliation if you disclose them.

We often feel embarrassed to talk about what we want. Not the easy wants ("I want to go to that new restaurant," "I want a new jacket," "I want to go on a trip"), but the personal wants that come from deep down, where we feel most vulnerable ("I want you to say sweet things to me," "I want to be more affectionate with you," "I want to be around you more"). Most of us grew up feeling ashamed of these wants. However, the more you communicate on this level, the more in touch you will be with yourself, and the more authentic you will be as a person. When you communicate with your partner on this personal level, many of the trivial issues between you vanish. And as inconsequential matters are minimized, you become more concerned with what is really important.

Listening to Your Partner

When you enter into a conversation, realize that you have very little awareness of what your partner really thinks and feels. You may think you do because you recognize an expression that always appears on your partner's face when he or she is hurt or angry. But until you have actually heard your partner, you know almost nothing. As the saying goes, we can listen, but that doesn't mean we've heard. Only when we listen with unconditional interest in understanding the thoughts and feelings of the person who is talking can we truly get to know that person.

Listen with your heart. When your partner tells you about an incident, try to put yourself in your partner's place. When you feel what your partner is feeling, you gain a sense of your partner as a human being who has personal pain and struggles like everyone else's. You gain a new perspective. When you feel for your partner's issues, your own personal overreactions become less significant. Giving advice or being judgmental suddenly seems condescending and patronizing. Acting hurt or victimized seems childish and self-indulgent. You are able to see your partner as a separate person for whom you care deeply as he or she copes with issues in life.

It is not enough to listen silently. It is helpful to demonstrate that you are hearing what your partner is saying. Say aloud what you sense your partner is feeling. If your reflection is not accurate, your partner can correct you. All along, you can make adjustments until you have a true understanding of what your partner is trying to communicate. Accurately reflecting what your partner has said makes your partner feel seen by you.

Reflecting on What You Have Learned from Your Conversation

Toward the conclusion of a conversation, it is helpful to review what you have learned about yourself, your partner, and your relationship. If you and your partner discuss what each of you has learned, you can identify the issues and reactions that tend to lead to trouble between you. You will have a better idea of what to look out for and avoid in the future. And if you do get into trouble, you will be able to recognize what is happening and deal with it more effectively.

Your critical inner voice will try to undermine your communication. It will warn you not to reveal yourself: *Don't tell him this—he'll use it against you later.* It will try to make you feel ashamed: *She'll lose all respect for you.* It will accuse you of being boring or tell you that your partner isn't interested: *You're just babbling, and he's not even listening.* It will predict a negative outcome: *When she finds this out, she's going to leave you.* It will try to make you suspicious of your partner: *What does he really mean? Is he implying something about you?* or *Is she telling the truth? Is she manipulating you?* While you're communicating, make every effort to be fully present with your partner. Look into your partner's eyes while you are talking and listening. When you maintain this level of personal connection, there will be less room in your head for attacks from your critical inner voice.

Much of the confusion and conflict between you and your partner can be clarified with the help of the insight and understanding that come from this type of communicating, along with the empathy and compassion that accompany it. Your deeper awareness of each other eliminates many of your misconceptions, misinterpretations, and miscommunications. What remains is a clearer picture of yourself, your partner, and the reality of your relationship. Remember Oliver, from chapter 8, who wanted to counteract his tendency to use withdrawal and overwork as a means of pulling away from Dom:

> Oliver had become so caught up in work that he went a week barely speaking to Dom—and, worst of all, Oliver hadn't even noticed. This worried him. He decided to improve his way of communicating so that this could never happen again.
>
> At first it was hard for Oliver to open up about himself, even though Dom was interested and encouraging. When Oliver did, he felt vulnerable, as if he were letting Dom get too close. Oliver asked Dom about himself, and he listened to Dom with genuine interest and curiosity.
>
> In the beginning, Oliver had to battle his critical inner voice: *What are you doing? It's better not to share this much of yourself. There are things better kept to yourself.* But as Oliver persisted, his critical inner voice subsided, and he began to cherish the developing intimacy and trust between himself and Dom.

Journal Exercise 10.2. Your Thoughts About How You Communicate with Your Partner

Reflect on the following questions, and record your thoughts in your journal.

- Do I speak about myself as personally and openly as I would like to?

- Do I listen to my partner as carefully and compassionately as I would like to?

- After a conversation, do I take time to reflect on what I have learned about myself, my partner, and our relationship?

- Am I aware of what is being communicated nonverbally?

- Am I ever intimidating in conversations with my partner?

- Do I relate in ways that are childish or parental?

Dealing with Anger Constructively

One of the challenges that all couples face is dealing with anger. This applies to expressing your own anger as well as hearing and responding to your partner's anger. Everyone gets angry, no matter how psychologically mature and how open and undefended during interactions. Anger is a natural part of everyday life. In a close relationship, you need the skills to deal with your own anger as well as your partner's so that it will not have a destructive impact on your relationship.

To be able to express your anger in a way that is constructive, you first need to understand anger. Anger is an emotion that most people misperceive and have learned very little about. For one thing, anger is not a negative emotion. Some people regard it as bad or immoral and feel that becoming angry makes them a bad person. Others believe that anger is the opposite of love and feel that expressions of anger have no place in close personal relationships. Still another common yet incorrect belief is that being angry with someone implies that you are accusing that person of wrongdoing. But it is not bad or mean to be angry. Angry feelings are neither right nor wrong. As the Dalai Lama wisely observed, "Generally speaking, if a human being never shows anger, then I think something's wrong. He's not right in the brain" ("10 Questions for His Holiness the Dalai Lama" n.d.).

There are two fundamental guidelines for dealing with anger:

1. All angry feelings are acceptable and should be allowed free rein in your consciousness.

2. The same freedom does *not* apply to your actions—you are accountable for your actions and bear full responsibility for all of your behavior and responses in relation to others.

How to Express Anger in a Close Relationship

To have a successful relationship, you have to develop the ability to engage in an honest exchange of angry feelings. You develop this ability so you can heal the rupture in your intimacy, not so you can prove yourself right or your partner wrong. Your aim is to communicate any emotional pain you may be experiencing, to clarify the ways in which you feel distressed, and to ask for what you want. Your goal is to seek relief from agitated, heated emotions and bring about a desired change.

You have to communicate your anger matter-of-factly, simply saying what you are angry about in a strong manner, without acting punishing. Verbalizing your frustration in a harsh tone, or expressing your wants as demands, often provokes an angry response that escalates the situation. Be specific about the reasons you are angry. For example, describe your frustration, hurt, or disappointment. Avoid implying that your partner is responsible for your angry feelings.

Final advice: When you are so angry that you want to call your partner every hurtful name in the book, don't. When you want to make your partner squirm, don't. When you want nothing more than to inflict pain and make your partner's life pure hell, don't. You can talk about these feelings without acting them out: "I want to hurt you. I want to humiliate you. I want to cause you pain! I want to say horrible, mean things about you! I want to punish you! I feel like I want to make your life miserable!" But do not act these feelings out.

The critical inner voice tends to become more active when you get angry. Once your temper starts to flare, the voice will suddenly be full of advice and have a lot to say about you and your partner: *Are you going to let him treat you like that?* or *You can't trust her!* or *He's making a fool of you!* Acknowledge your critical inner voice when it intensifies your anger and alienates you from your partner. Becoming aware of your critical inner voice and its cynical attitudes can help you prevent such thoughts from fueling your anger and being translated into destructive actions.

How to Respond to Anger

There are lessons to be learned about responding to anger that are helpful to couples. One is that when someone gets angry at us, we all have the same knee-jerk reaction—we feel angry in turn and want to defend ourselves. Our reaction is quick and irrational: "Don't get angry at me! Shut your mouth! I don't want to hear what you are saying!" This response is natural. Quite simply, anger begets anger. And also, quite simply, this response doesn't have to be dramatic. Acknowledge your feeling of anger to yourself, and then get down to the business of dealing with the issues: "Okay, now what is it that she is saying? What's going on here?" If you skip over your initial anger, it may continue to smolder and can have a damaging effect on your communication with your partner.

Remain respectful of your partner, even in your anger. Resist using the underhanded tactic so popular with many couples—saying the exact thing that will get under your partner's skin and set him or her off. On the occasions when your partner uses this tactic with you, you can resist taking the bait. You can strive to remain who you want to be, regardless of how your partner is acting. When you do not allow yourself to be provoked into being someone you do not like, you strengthen your personal power. Another benefit is that you avoid saying the kind of hurtful thing that can cause lasting damage to your partner and your relationship.

Having anger directed toward you can activate your critical inner voice. You may be considering the content of the feedback from your partner objectively, but on a deeper, emotional level your critical inner voice may be attacking you. Regardless of whether the anger directed toward you is harsh or mild, fair or unfair, certain statements can trigger an attack from your critical inner voice. When this happens, you are no longer relating to your partner; instead, you are engaging in an internal dialogue with your critical inner voice, defending yourself against it and reacting to its attacks and hostile views. For example, if your partner says, "I was disappointed that you weren't more affectionate the other night," your critical inner voice may step in and take over: *You are a cold, unfeeling person. Your heart is made of ice!* And then you fire back at your partner: "Are you saying that I'm cold? How dare you say that I don't have a heart!" When you are aware that your critical inner voice is causing you to overreact, you can listen and respond to what your partner is actually saying.

How to Defuse an Argument

There are times when an argument is escalating and there is no resolution in sight. And some disagreements just cannot be resolved. It is possible to unilaterally disarm and simply stop fighting because you value your relationship more than winning your point. You can appreciate that you and your partner are two separate people, with two separate minds, and that you will see any number of events or situations from your two different standpoints. You can acknowledge an impasse and live comfortably with it. Once your fight has de-escalated, you can even work together, with respect for your different positions, to negotiate a solution that both of you can live with. You can approach the problem as a team and—together, with compromise, flexibility, and some creativity—come up with a workable arrangement.

The critical inner voice does not like unilateral disarmament, and it will tell you so: *What are you doing? You're letting him off the hook. You're just rolling over and letting him win* or *Stand your ground—don't give an inch. You're letting her gain control. You're letting her walk all over you.* As you know very well by now, the critical inner voice supports your defenses. Therefore, it sees reconciliation as an act of weakness, whereas in fact reconciliation is an act of vulnerability, love, and strength. Recall Henry and Catherine, from chapter 4—when they became embroiled in a conflict that they could not resolve, Henry used unilateral disarmament to ease the tension between them and help them both arrive at a mutually acceptable solution:

> Henry wanted Catherine and their son, Billy, to join him on a hike. But Catherine didn't enjoy hiking. Besides, she said, Henry had friends who were happy to go hiking with him, and Billy was only a year old—too young for a serious hike.
>
> "But you told me you don't want me to be isolated," Henry protested, "and now you're saying you won't come with me!"
>
> Catherine lost no time firing back. "I can't stand hiking! How many times do I have to tell you?"
>
> Henry pressed on. "But hiking is something I really enjoy! I always imagined sharing it with you and Billy. Can't you see how important this is to me?"

"I understand that," Catherine said. "And I'm sorry to disappoint you. I really am. I'm also sorry that I don't like to hike. It's beautiful to be out in nature, and I appreciate that. But hiking is unpleasant for me. My back ends up hurting, and I feel bad."

"I know," Henry said. "But I wish you'd try harder."

"And *I* wish *you'd* stop pressuring me!"

Henry and Catherine realized they had reached a stalemate, and Henry decided to disarm. He reached out to Catherine.

"I don't want to fight with you about this," he said. "In the overall scheme of things, it isn't a big deal."

Catherine softened. "Thanks. I don't want to fight with you, either. And I know you understand that hiking hurts my back. Maybe we can work out a compromise. What if Billy and I join you at the trailhead after the hike, and we can all hang out together at the campground?"

Journal Exercise 10.3. Your Thoughts About How You Deal with Anger

Reflect on the following questions, and record your thoughts in your journal.

- Am I accepting of and comfortable with my anger?

- Do I have any misconceptions about anger? Do I consider anger to be bad or mean or not normal?

- Do I swallow my anger and push it down?

- Do I ever blow up?

- Do I allow myself to feel all of my anger?

- Do I maintain control over my actions so that I don't act out my anger?

- When I express my anger, do I focus on talking about myself and my current feelings?

- Do I ever define or attack my partner?

- Am I ever parental or judgmental?

- Do I ever exaggerate or make generalizations? Do I drag in the past or stew about the future?

- Do I ever unilaterally disarm to defuse an argument?

- Am I able to collaborate with my partner when we reach a stalemate?

- What is the critical inner voice that fuels my anger?

The Act of Loving

No relationship can exist in a vacuum. The *act* of loving is more gratifying for both the lover and the beloved than the *state* of being in love. That state is passive. It easily dissolves into an internal fantasy about being in love, and its passivity encourages your critical inner voice. But the act of loving discourages that voice. The act of loving involves various types of real behavior (such as offering emotional and physical acts of affection; expressing tenderness, compassion, and sensitivity to your partner's needs; sharing activities and interests; maintaining honest exchanges of personal thoughts and feelings) that will keep a close relationship alive and vital.

There are three simple steps that make up the act of loving:

1. Acknowledging and accepting your partner's loving actions

2. Being grateful and expressing your gratitude

3. Giving back with actions of your own

As we develop the ability to accept love with dignity and return love with appreciation, we find ourselves actively involved in being in love rather than falling into a passive state of fantasizing about being in love.

Acknowledging and Accepting Your Partner's Loving Actions

The first step is to recognize and accept the loving actions coming from your partner. This is much more difficult than it sounds because most of us lack full awareness of what is given to us. We tend to see our partner in terms of what we want from him or her or what we should be getting from him or her.

To gain perspective, step back from your partner. As you stand apart, get a feeling for yourself as a separate, independent person, perfectly capable of functioning on your own. The world doesn't owe you anything; and, in spite of life's disappointments and frustrations, you are a victim of no one. You are just you, alone. Now take a look at your partner, apart from you. Separate from anything you may expect, want, or demand from your partner. Separate from any role your partner may be fulfilling in relation to you. Like you, your partner is a person, alone.

Once you are able to experience yourself and your partner from this vantage point—seeing the two of you as two discrete individuals—look at what your partner is giving you. Don't look for grandiose gestures of love and devotion. Don't look for what you think your partner ought to be doing for you. Look for real, everyday acts of thoughtfulness, sensitivity, and kindness. Look for unique acts of giving that are an expression of your partner's nature and sensitivity to your nature. Partners hurt each other by overlooking simple acts of love. However, when you acknowledge your partner's acts of love, you accept the love your partner is offering to you.

Being Grateful and Expressing Your Gratitude

Once you have acknowledged and accepted what your partner is giving you, the next step is to be grateful and express your gratitude to your partner. But don't rely on the occasional extravagant or effusive expression of gratitude. Instead, express your gratitude to your partner whenever you experience tender feelings of thankfulness because he or she has extended kindness, sensitivity, or generosity to you.

Giving Back with Actions of Your Own

Once you have acknowledged, accepted, felt gratitude, and expressed your gratitude for what your partner is giving you, the final step is to give back to your partner. But giving back to your partner is about being attuned to your partner as a person, separate from you and your relationship. Giving back to your partner involves, first of all, your awareness that you are two different people with your own individual traits, interests, and desires, and it's this awareness that attunes you to what your partner personally wants and needs. Therefore, the final step is the act of responding to your partner's personal needs with actions that are highly sensitive. Because this personal level of giving is such a profound expression of yourself, the more wholeheartedly you give back to your partner, the more fully you realize who *you* are. Expressing your love in this manner enriches both your lives.

Your critical inner voice will try to sabotage your loving exchanges with your partner. It will influence you to overlook a loving gesture: *He never demonstrates his love for you. I don't see any signs of it.* It will belittle your partner's loving responses: *You call that loving? It's nothing. You deserve more than that.* It will make fun of you when you acknowledge something your partner has given you: *You are so pitiful! You're practically groveling.* It will ridicule the exchanges between you: *You two lovebirds are so mushy, it nauseates me. I can practically hear the violins in the background.* But when you ignore your critical inner voice and continue to be loving, the voice will weaken and fade, and you will triumph. Let's look back in on Jack and Sonia, whom we met in chapter 9; after Sonia's father died, Jack wanted to stop pushing her away and instead be loving toward her:

> Jack reacted so intensely to his feelings about even the
> thought of one day losing his father that he stopped being able
> to empathize with what Sonia was experiencing in the wake of
> her own father's recent death. When Jack became aware of
> this change in his behavior toward Sonia, he saw once again
> how available she still was to him, in spite of her grief. Jack
> thanked Sonia for her kindness, and she was touched not only

by what he said but also by his tender way of speaking to her. Their exchanges quelled the critical inner voice in Jack that had been arousing his anxiety about death. More important, these exchanges helped Jack and Sonia get closer at a time when being close especially mattered.

Journal Exercise 10.4. Reflecting on What You Have Learned

Now that you have come to the end of this book, take some time to go back and read through all your journal exercises. As you review them, pay attention to the defenses you have identified, and to how your critical inner voice encourages them. Reflect on how you've confronted your critical inner voice, and on the plans of action you created to counter it. Then consider the following questions, and write your thoughts about them in your journal.

- Do I still experience attacks from my critical inner voice?

- If so, is my critical inner voice still as strong? Stronger? Or does the strength of my critical inner voice depend on the circumstances? If so, what circumstances make it stronger or weaker?

- Is my critical inner voice plaguing me with anything today that I wasn't aware of before?

- If so, what is my critical inner voice saying?

- Have I become stronger in confronting my critical inner voice? Weaker? Or does my ability to confront my critical inner voice depend on the circumstances? If so, what circumstances make me stronger or weaker in confronting my critical inner voice?

- Am I aware now of ways to confront my critical inner voice that I wasn't aware of initially?

- If so, what are they?

- Have I changed the behavior that I planned to challenge?

- Were some of my action plans easier for me to implement than others? If so, which action plans were harder for me to implement?

- Am I thinking of any action plans now that I didn't think of initially?

- If so, what are they? How will I implement them?

It is beneficial to repeat this process regularly. Reviewing your journal exercises keeps you focused on your goals for improving your relationship and helps you evaluate your progress. If you are having difficulty, you can identify the critical inner voice that is causing the problem, verbalize it, reflect on its message, confront the voice, devise a plan of action for countering it, and then implement your plan. And updating your journal will encourage you to think about new ways in which the critical inner voice may be trying to undermine your efforts to overcome your internal barriers to love and have more intimacy and romance in your relationship.

A Few Final Words

It is empowering to know that the ability to solve a problem in your relationship lies with you and your capacity to accept and tolerate love. But this knowledge is also disturbing. It is upsetting to realize that love can make you feel vulnerable, and that it can challenge your old identity or trigger guilt. It is painful to see that giving and receiving love can make you increasingly aware of your aloneness. It is unnerving to discover that falling in love means coming face to face with your internal enemy, the critical inner voice. It is unsettling to acknowledge that with real joy comes real pain, and that love stirs up your fear of loss and your anxiety about death.

But when you understand your defenses, and how love threatens them, you can deal with your negative reactions to intimacy. When you know how your critical inner voice supports your defenses and influences you to push love away, you can use Voice Therapy to take the actions that will allow love to thrive. You can maintain intimacy in your relationship by continuing to use this knowledge and the tools you have found in this book. Whenever you and your partner hit a rocky patch, you can apply what you have learned to get back on course.

We would like to end the book with some personal words of advice and encouragement.

From Tamsen

- *Be courageous.* It takes courage to change your defensive behavior, and to sweat out the anxiety that this change process may arouse in you. With courage, you can face and overcome the critical inner voice that tries to sabotage you. And with courage, you can create a better life and a more gratifying relationship.

- *Be optimistic.* Being optimistic is a notable relationship skill—it's a notable life skill, for that matter. It's valuable to look for the good in people and situations, and especially in yourself, your partner, and your relationship. Growing cynical only leaves you feeling miserable and disillusioned. Keeping an optimistic outlook will fortify you and lead to positive outcomes. As the Dalai Lama is reported to have said (Jezek-Arriaga 2017, 144), "Choose to be optimistic, it feels better."

- *Take action.* Never forget that love is not just a noun. It's also a verb—an action. The source of your greatest power and freedom in life is your ability to choose the actions that you are going to take. If you want a close and intimate relationship, and if you value having love in your life, take action, and behave consistently in a loving manner.

From Robert

- *Give it your all.* When you are in a relationship, give it your all. Don't hold back. Go for broke. Dare to love! Don't waste an opportunity by being cautious and self-protective. Daring to love will give you the best chance for the best outcome—a loving and gratifying relationship.

- *Give yourself a break.* Have compassion for yourself, especially as you confront your defenses that interfere with love. Whatever your limitations and challenges in loving and relating to someone close to you, always remember that you came by them honestly. No one is *innately* lacking or incapable of loving. You can have compassion for the ways in which you have been hurt, and for how they are impacting you in your romantic relationship. You can be kind and patient with yourself as you go about changing the defenses that arose from how you were hurt.

- *Have a sense of humor!* A sense of humor can be a lifesaver in a relationship. The ability to laugh at yourself, and even at life, allows you to maintain a proper perspective while dealing with sensitive issues that arise within your relationship. Partners who are playful and tease each other can use humor to defuse a potentially volatile situation. A good sense of humor eases the tense moments between partners. Plus, it always feels good to have fun with someone!

From Both of Us

- *Believe in love.* In spite of the violence and unrest in the world, and regardless of the abuse that individuals are capable of inflicting on their fellow human beings, love continues to be universally acknowledged as the essential life force. As Robert observes in *Sex and Love in Intimate Relationships,* "When love is sincere and real, it reaches spiritual proportions that give value and meaning to life" (R. W. Firestone, L. A. Firestone, & Catlett 2006, 39).

- *Love is worth believing in.* Love is worth fighting for. Love is worth the personal challenge. No other endeavor offers higher rewards.

Acknowledgments

We, Tamsen and Robert, are thankful to the many people who helped this book come to be. To Jo Barrington and Susan Short for their editing skills, to Lisa Firestone and Joyce Catlett for their suggestions, and to Joyce Catlett for the referencing.

We appreciate Matthew McKay of New Harbinger Publications for going to bat for us. We are also indebted to the rest of the team at New Harbinger, who generously offered their support and expertise all along. And we are beholden to Xavier Callahan for working her magic on the book.

Since I, Tamsen, had the idea of writing the book, I would like to personally thank my family and friends for supporting me and cheering me on throughout the project. And thanks to every one of these people for disagreeing with the critical inner voice that was telling me I had no business writing a book. But mostly I am grateful to Robert, for many things. For his psychological ideas and the many other books he has written. For my having been able to work closely with him over the past thirty years. For his abiding belief in me and what I am capable of, which continues to surprise and inspire me. For our children. For our life together over the last forty years. For his love for me. For being someone I can love so much. And for writing this book with me.

References

Ainsworth, M. D. S. 1989. "Attachments Beyond Infancy." *American Psychologist* 44 (4): 709–16.

Ainsworth, M. D. S., M. C. Blehar, E. Waters, and S. Wall. 1978. *Patterns of Attachment: A Psychological Study of the Strange Situation.* Hillsdale, NJ: Erlbaum.

Bandura, A. 1975. *Social Learning Through Imitation.* New York: Holt, Rinehart, and Winston.

Bandura, A., and B. H. Walters. 1963. *Social Learning and Personality Development.* New York: Holt, Rinehart, and Winston.

Baumeister, R. F., E. Bratslavsky, C. Finkenauer, and K. D. Vohs. 2001. "Bad Is Stronger Than Good." *Review of General Psychology* 5: 323–70.

Bowlby, J. 1982. *Attachment and Loss.* Vol. 1, *Attachment* (2nd ed.). New York: Basic Books.

Bowlby, J. 1988. *A Secure Base: Parent-Child Attachment and Healthy Human Development.* New York: Basic Books.

Branfman, F. 1972. *Voices from the Plain of Jars: Life under an Air War.* New York: Harper & Row.

Briere, J. N. 1992. *Child Abuse Trauma: Theory and Treatment of the Lasting Effects.* Newbury Park, CA: Sage.

Brown, B. 2010. "The Power of Vulnerability." Filmed June 2010 in Houston, TX. TED video, 20:19. https://www.ted.com/talks/brene_brown_on _vulnerability.

Brown, B. 2012. *Daring Greatly: How the Courage to be Vulnerable Transforms the Way We Live, Love, Parent, and Lead.* New York: Avery.

Chess, S., and A. Thomas. 1986. *Temperament in Clinical Practice.* New York: Guilford Press.

Ciotti, G. n.d. "Transparency vs. Infotainment." Sparring Mind. http://www .sparringmind.com/transparency-vs-infotainment. Accessed August 25, 2017.

Cozolino, L. 2006. *The Neuroscience of Human Relationships: Attachment and the Developing Social Brain*. New York: Norton.

Cozolino, L. 2015. *Why Therapy Works: Using Our Mind to Change Our Brain*. New York: Norton.

Daily Mail. 2014. "So What Is Love?" December 18, 2014. http://www.daily mail.co.uk/femail/article-2879951/So-love-one-2014-s-popular-web -searches-needs-Google-experts-enchanting-thought-provoking -answers.html.

Dickinson, E. 1955. "That It Will Never Come Again." In *Poems of Emily Dickinson*. Edited by Thomas H. Johnson. Cambridge, MA: Harvard University Press.

Doidge, N. 2007. *The Brain That Changes Itself*. New York: Penguin.

The Economist. 2014. "Obituary: Fred Branfman: An Inconvenient Truth." October 17, 2014. https://www.economist.com/news/obituary/21625649 -fred-branfman-exposer-americas-secret-war-laos-died-september-24th -aged-72.

Firestone, R. W. 1984. "A Concept of the Primary Fantasy Bond: A Developmental Perspective." *Psychotherapy* 21: 218–25.

Firestone, R. W. 1985. *The Fantasy Bond: Structure of Psychological Defenses*. Santa Barbara, CA: The Glendon Association.

Firestone, R. W. 1987. "The 'Voice': The Dual Nature of Guilt Reactions." *American Journal of Psychoanalysis* 47: 211–29.

Firestone, R. W. 1994. "Psychological Defenses Against Death Anxiety." In *Death Anxiety Handbook: Research, Instrumentation, and Application*. Edited by R. A. Niemeyer. Washington, DC: Taylor & Francis.

Firestone, R. W. 1997a. *Combating Destructive Thought Processes: Voice Therapy and Separation Theory*. Santa Barbara, CA: The Glendon Association.

Firestone, R. W. 1997b. *Suicide and the Inner Voice: Risk Assessment, Treatment, and Case Management*. Santa Barbara, CA: The Glendon Association.

Firestone, R. W. 2013a. "Why Do So Many People Respond Negatively to Being Loved?" PsychAlive: Psychology for Everyday Life. https://www .psychalive.org/why-people-respond-negatively-to-being-loved. Accessed August 28, 2017.

Firestone, R. W. 2013b. "Why Do We Hate Love?" *The Human Experience* (blog), *Psychology Today*, October 29, 2013. https://www.psychology today.com/blog/the-human-experience/201310/why-do-we-hate-love.

Firestone, R. W., and J. Catlett. 1999. *Fear of Intimacy*. Washington, DC: American Psychological Association.

Firestone, R. W., and J. Catlett. 2009a. *Beyond Death Anxiety: Achieving Life-Affirming Death Awareness*. New York: Springer.

Firestone, R. W., and J. Catlett. 2009b. *The Ethics of Interpersonal Relationships*. London: Karnac.

Firestone, R. W., L. Firestone, and J. Catlett. 2002. *Conquer Your Critical Inner Voice: A Revolutionary Program to Counter Negative Thoughts and Live Free from Imagined Limitations*. Oakland, CA: New Harbinger.

Firestone, R. W., L. A. Firestone, and J. Catlett. 2006. *Sex and Love in Intimate Relationships*. Washington, DC: American Psychological Association.

Fromm, E. 1956. *The Art of Loving*. New York: Bantam Books.

Garbarino, J. 1995. *Raising Children in a Socially Toxic Environment*. San Francisco: Jossey-Bass.

Gibran, K. 1996. *The Prophet*. Hertfordshire, UK: Wordsworth Editions.

Gilbert, P. 1989. *Human Nature and Suffering*. Hove, UK: Erlbaum.

Gilligan, C. 1982. *In a Different Voice: Psychological Theory and Women's Development*. Cambridge, MA: Harvard University Press.

Gove, W. R., and M. Hughes. 1980. "Reexamining the Ecological Fallacy: A Study in Which Aggregate Data Are Critical in Investigating the Pathological Effects of Living Alone." *Social Forces* 58: 1157–77.

Greenberg, L. S. 2002. *Emotion-Focused Therapy: Coaching Clients to Work Through Their Feelings*. Washington, DC: American Psychological Association.

Greenberg, L. S., and R. N. Goldman. 2008. *Emotion-Focused Couples Therapy: The Dynamics of Emotion, Love, and Power*. Washington, DC: American Psychological Association.

Heckler, R. A. 1994. *Waking Up, Alive: The Descent, the Suicide Attempt, and the Return to Life*. New York: Ballantine.

Hoffman, S. I., and S. Strauss. 1985. "The Development of Children's Concepts of Death." *Death Studies* 9: 469–82.

Jezek-Arriaga, S. 2017. *Nourish to Flourish*. Bloomington, IN: Balboa Press.

Kastenbaum, R. 2000. *The Psychology of Death*, 3rd ed. New York: Springer.

Kolb, B., G. Robbin, and T. E. Robinson. 2003. "Brain Plasticity and Behavior." *Current Directions in Psychological Science* 12: 1–5.

Kolb, D. A. 1984. *Experiential Learning*. Englewood Cliffs, NJ: Prentice-Hall.

Laing, R. D. 1971. *Self and Others*. Harmondsworth, UK: Penguin.

Lamb, M. E., and C. Lewis. 2004. "The Development and Significance of Father-Child Relationships in Two-Parent Families." In *The Role of the Father in Child Development*, 4th ed. Edited by M. E. Lamb. New York: Wiley.

Lane, R. D., L. Ryan, L. Nadel, and L. Greenberg. 2015. "Memory Reconsolidation, Emotional Arousal, and the Process of Change in Psychotherapy: New Insights from Brain Science." *Behavioral and Brain Sciences* 38: 1–64.

Lickerman, A. 2012. *The Undefeated Mind: On the Science of Constructing an Indestructible Self*. Deerfield, FL: Health Communications.

Main, M., and E. Hesse. 1990. "Parents' Unresolved Traumatic Experiences Are Related to Infant Disorganized Attachment Status: Is Frightened and/or Frightening Parental Behavior the Linking Mechanism?" In *Attachment in the Preschool Years: Theory, Research, and Intervention*. Edited by M. T. Greenberg, D. Cicchetti, and E. M. Cummings. Chicago: University of Chicago Press.

Maslow, A. H. 1968. *Toward a Psychology of Being*, 2nd ed. New York: Van Nostrand Reinhold.

Maslow, A. H. 1971. *The Farther Reaches of Human Nature*. Harmondsworth, UK: Penguin.

Meaney, M. J. 2010. "Epigenetics and the Biological Definition of Gene-Environment Interactions." *Child Development* 81: 41–79.

Mikulincer, M., and P. R. Shaver. 2016. *Attachment in Adulthood: Structure, Dynamics, and Change*, 2nd ed. New York: Guilford Press.

Perry, B. D. 2001. "Violence and Childhood: How Persisting Fear Can Alter the Developing Child's Brain." In *Textbook of Child and Adolescent Forensic Psychiatry*. Edited by D. Schetky and E. Benedek. Washington, DC: American Psychiatric Press.

Perry, B. D. 2002. "Childhood Experience and the Expression of Genetic Potential: What Childhood Neglect Tells Us About Nature and Nurture." *Brain and Mind* 3: 79–100.

Plutchik, R. 2000. *Emotions in the Practice of Psychotherapy: Clinical Implications of Affect Theories*. Washington, DC: American Psychological Association.

Schore, A. N. 1994. *Affect Regulation and the Origin of the Self: The Neurobiology of Emotional Development*. Hillsdale, NJ: Erlbaum.

Schore, A. N. 2003a. *Affect Regulation and Disorders of the Self.* New York: Norton.

Schore, A. N. 2003b. *Affect Regulation and the Repair of the Self.* New York: Norton.

Schore, A. N. 2009. "Relational Trauma and the Developing Right Brain: An Interface of Psychoanalytic Self Psychology and Neuroscience." In *Self and Systems: Explorations in Contemporary Self Psychology.* Annals of the New York Academy of Sciences, vol. 1159. Edited by W. J. Coburn and N. Van Der Heide. Boston: Blackwell.

Seiden, R. H. 1984. "Death in the West: A Regional Analysis of the Youthful Suicide Rate." *Western Journal of Medicine* 140: 969–73.

Shapiro, D. 2000. *Dynamics of Character: Self-Regulation in Psychopathology.* New York: Basic Books.

Shenk, J. W. 2006. *Lincoln's Melancholy: How Depression Challenged a President and Fueled His Greatness.* New York: Mariner Books.

Siegel, D. J. 1999. *The Developing Mind: Toward a Neurobiology of Interpersonal Experience.* New York: Guilford Press.

Siegel, D. J., and M. Hartzell. 2003. *Parenting from the Inside Out: How a Deeper Self-Understanding Can Help You Raise Children Who Thrive.* New York: Tarcher.

"10 Questions for His Holiness the Dalai Lama: *Time* Magazine Interview." n.d. His Holiness the 14th Dalai Lama of Tibet. https://www.dalailama .com/messages/transcripts-and-interviews/10-questions-time-magazine . Accessed August 25, 2017.

Vaish, A., T. Grossmann, and A. Woodward. 2008. "Not All Emotions Are Created Equal: The Negativity Bias in Social-Emotional Development." *Psychological Bulletin* 134: 383–403.

Welling, H. 2012. "Transformative Emotional Sequence: Towards a Common Principle of Change." *Journal of Psychotherapy Integration* 22: 109–36.

Zull, J. E. 2004. "The Art of Changing the Brain: Teaching for Meaning." *Educational Leadership* 62: 68–72.

Tamsen Firestone is founder and editor-in-chief of www.psychalive .org, an online mental health resource visited by millions of people each year. She has also been principal editor for many of the books written by her husband, author and clinical psychologist Robert W. Firestone. Among these are *Fear of Intimacy, Conquer Your Critical Inner Voice*, and *Creating a Life of Meaning and Compassion*. Her work, including the PsychAlive website, speaks to the general public and provides easy-to-understand, practical steps that a person can follow to apply her husband's theories of human behavior in order to experience a more rewarding and fulfilling life. She lives in Santa Barbara, CA.

Robert W. Firestone, PhD, is a psychologist and author whose best-known books—*The Fantasy Bond, Voice Therapy, Combating Destructive Thought Processes*, and *Compassionate Child-Rearing*—outline a comprehensive theory on neurosis and human development. His studies on negative thought processes and their associated effect have led to the development of voice therapy, an advanced therapeutic methodology to uncover and contend with aspects of self-destructive and self-limiting behaviors. Recently, Firestone authored *Overcoming the Destructive Inner Voice*, a book of short stories inspired by his experiences as a psychotherapist.

Foreword writer **Leslie S. Greenberg, PhD**, is distinguished research professor emeritus of psychology at York University in Toronto, Ontario, Canada.

MORE BOOKS *from*
NEW HARBINGER PUBLICATIONS

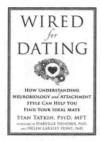
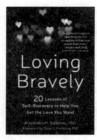